INSIGHT COMPACT GUIDE

ICELAND

Compact Guide: Iceland is the ultimate quick-reference guide to this fascinating destination. It tells you all you need to know about Iceland's attractions, from its glaciers and geothermal springs to its waterfalls and volcanoes, not forgetting its picturesque settlements and its lively capital, Reykjavík.

Compact Guides are produced by the editors of Insight Guides, whose books have set the standard for visual travel guides since 1970. Packed with information, arranged in easy-to-follow routes, and lavishly illustrated with photographs, this book not only steers you round Iceland but also gives you fascinating insights into local life.

APA PUBLICATIONS

Part of the Langenscheidt Publishing Group

Insight Compact Guide: Iceland

Written by: Hans Klüche
English version by: Paul Fletcher
Photography by: Britta Jaschinski/Apa
Except for: Icelandic Tourist Board 39B. Icelandic Tourist Board/Photo: BKN Studios
9T. Icelandic Tourist Board/Photo: Randall Hyman 20/21, 54B, 64, 66T, 72B, 86T,
88, 91B, 111, 112. Icelandic Tourist Board/Photo: Ruth Gundahl Madsen 46B, 54T,
56B, 67. Icelandic Tourist Board/Photo: Thierry des Ouches 70. Icelandic Tourist
Board/Photo: Frederic Reglain 9B, 60B, Icelandic Tourist Board/Photo: Dieter
Schweizer 6, 11, 12, 38, 43T&B, 44, 50B, 53B, 65B, 66B, 69B, 71B, 86B, 123. Icelandic Tourist Board/Photo: Walter Sommerhalder 59T. Icelandic Tourist Board/Photo:
www.adventure.is 97B, 108. Hans Klüche 36, 46T, 47, 50T, 56T, 57, 59B, 60T, 61,
63T, 65T, 68B, 69T, 71T, 72B, 73, 74 ,77, 78, 79, 80, 81, 83T, 84, 85, 89, 90, 91T,
92B, 93, 94, 95, 97T. Morunbaladid/Arni Saeberg 103B. Lance Price/Apa 7B, 39T, 42,
45, 49, 52, 53T, 55B, 58, 62, 63B, 75, 83M&B, 87B, 96B, 99T. Gerhard Steidl 99B
Cover picture by: Wilfried Krecichwost/Stone/Getty Images
Design: Clare Peel
Picture Editor: Hilary Genin
Maps: Polyglott/Huber

CONTACTING THE EDITORS: As every effort is made to provide accurate
information in this publication, we would appreciate it if readers would
call our attention to any errors and omissions by contacting:
Apa Publications, PO Box 7910, London SE1 1WE, England.
Fax: (44 20) 7403 0290; e-mail: insight@apaguide.co.uk

Information has been obtained from sources believed to be reliable,
but its accuracy and completeness, and the opinions based thereon,
are not guaranteed.

© 2009 APA Publications GmbH & Co. Verlag KG Singapore Branch, Singapore.

First Edition 1995; Second Edition 2006; Reprinted 2009
Printed in Singapore by Insight Print Services (Pte) Ltd
Original edition © Polyglott-Verlag Dr Bolte KG, Munich

Worldwide distribution enquiries:
APA Publications GmbH & Co. Verlag KG (Singapore Branch)
38 Joo Koon Road, Singapore 628990
Tel: (65) 6865-1600, Fax: (65) 6861-6438

Distributed in the UK & Ireland by:
GeoCenter International Ltd
Meridian House, Churchill Way West
Basingstoke, Hampshire RG21 6YR
Tel: (44 1256) 817987, Fax: (44 1256) 817988

Distributed in the United States by:
Langenscheidt Publishers, Inc.
36-36 33rd Street 4th Floor
Long Island City, New York 11106
Tel: (1 718) 784-0055, Fax: (1 718) 784-0640

w w w . i n s i g h t g u i d e s . c o m

Introduction

Top Ten Sights 4
A Young Country 7
Historical Highlights..18

Places

1 Reykjavík 22
2 The 'Golden Circle' around Reykjavík....................34
3 Reykjavík to Akureyri..42
4 Akureyri to Mývatn...47
5 Iceland's East and South 60
6 Snæfellsnes and the Westfjords..............................77
7 Crossing the Central Highlands 91
8 Askja and Kverjökull 95

Culture

Literature and Music...99
Festivals and Events 102

Travel Tips

Food and Drink..105
Nightlife 107
Active Holidays...108
Practical Information...109
Accommodation 119

Index 128
Useful Phrases......................................Inside back cover

△ **Hveravellir (p93)**
This is an oasis within the cold desert, with deep pools of brilliant, near-boiling blue water and hot baths for soaking in.

△ **Jökulsárlón (p66)**
Extraordinary iceberg-studded glacial lagoon at the edge of Vatnajökull, the largest ice-cap in Europe

◁ **Snæfellsjökull (p78)**
This ice-capped volcano dominates the Snæfellsnes peninsula in western Iceland.

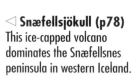

△ **Lake Mývatn (p51)**
At this beautiful lake you c●
witness abundant birdlife a●
spectacular volcanic activity●

◁ **Dettifoss (p57)**
In Jökulsárgljúfur National F●
in northeast Iceland, Dettifo●
Europe's largest waterfall ar●
Iceland's most awesome sig●

△ **Heimaey (p74)**
The cliffs of Heimaey island are teeming with birdlife: thousands of puffins, along with auk and storm petrels.

△ **Golden Circle (p34)**
Within easy reach of the capital, visit Strokkur geyser, Gullfoss waterfall and the parliament site at Þingvellir.

▽ **Hallgrímskirkja (p25)**
Reminiscent of Iceland's basalt rock formations, this modern church towers above Reykjavík.

△ **Blue Lagoon (p33)**
Relax in one of the country's most popular bathing pools, fed by springs rich in silica, salt and other elements.

▷ **Vík (p71)**
Just off the dramatic coast of Vík are the Reynisdrangur, fingers of black rock battered relentlessly by the sea.

A Young Country

A medieval manuscript tells the tale of Flóki Vilgerðarson, who in 864 attempted to settle on this remote island in the North Atlantic. Flóki's endeavours were thwarted because when he landed in spring and encountered idyllic conditions, he gave little thought to storing up provisions for the coming winter. When the cold months arrived, the cattle that he had brought with him perished through lack of feed. Before leaving the island he gave it the name of Iceland. Ironically, when Iceland's much icier neighbour to the west was discovered 100 years later, it was given the name of Greenland.

Opposite: Icelandic horse
Below: statue of Ingólfur Arnason, first settler on Iceland
Bottom: Viking armour

A good tenth of Iceland's surface area does justice to its name. Some 11,800 sq. km (4,556 sq. miles) is covered by glacial ice. But that is not the whole country by a long way. Other landscape features include volcanoes and fjords, meadows and barren wastes, hot springs and deafening waterfalls – Iceland is a country of great diversity. At first sight it seems raw, primeval and in some way incomplete, but on closer inspection it reveals a quiet and attractive face.

Unexpected colours and shapes can be found in newly formed lava, beside small streams or by hot pots, the thermal springs where mineral deposits have been shaped by nature into works of art. Iceland's flora also paints bright colours on to the island's canvas. Meadows, swathed with cotton grass like white clouds, are covered in violet carpets of Arctic fireweed amid the wastes of the otherwise barren uplands: when in flower a vivid, pioneer plant standing out against a background of scree that extends as far as the horizon.

Iceland cannot boast any famous historic monuments, world-ranking museums or grand castles, but that doesn't mean that the island has nothing cultural to offer. The museums that do document Icelandic art, history and people are well run and certainly worth a visit, if newcomers to the island are to find out more about this fascinating country and its inhabitants.

> **Amazing Icecap**
> Vatnajökull, up to 1km (3,300 ft) thick and 8,300 sq. km (3,200 sq. miles) in area, is not only Europe's largest icecap, it is also bigger than all the rest put together.

Human existence on the island of Iceland only points the way; it seems to have little impact on the scenery. Even Reykjavík, the island's undisputed capital, is characterised much more by the surrounding mountains than by the pervasive concrete architecture.

BACKGROUND AND GEOLOGY

Geologically, Iceland is one of the world's youngest nations. According to the theory that explains the development of the continents, back in the very early days of the earth's history, one large continental mass broke up into several continental plates and over a period lasting millions of years these plates drifted apart. The American and Eurasian (Europe and Asia) continents were once joined together and the mid-Atlantic ridge, upon which Iceland lies, is the seam between the two plates. It is visible in a number of places on the island, in the Þingvellir National Park *(see page 66)*, for example. The famous Almannagjá rift has, over the past 20 years, widened by 10cm (4 ins). It is thus possible to say that the east of Iceland belongs on the European side, the west of Iceland to the American side, and the middle is genuinely new land.

Bláa Loníð (Blue Lagoon)

However, as the island occupies such a key position in geological terms, there is the risk that eruptions of molten lava could take place at any time. Since the island was first settled in the 9th century, there have been at least 150 eruptions, some of which lasted for years. The Westman Islands (Vestmannaeyjar in Icelandic) off the south coast *(see page 50)* have been created exclusively by volcanic action.

The latest major eruption to take place here was in 1973, when totally without warning a new volcano erupted on the eastern side of Heimaey town on the main island. In 1963, to the south of the Westman Islands and to the accompaniment of columns of fire, clouds of ash and rumbles of thunder, a completely

new island emerged from the sea. It was called Surtsey after Surtr, the fire giant from Nordic mythology. The eruption lasted for three and a half years. By that time Surtsey had expanded to 2.5 sq. km (just under 1 sq. mile). Only scientists, keen to discover how new and isolated land is colonised by nature, have access to it.

Below: geothermal activity
Bottom: Gullfoss in winter

GEOGRAPHY

Iceland is an island republic in the North Atlantic. Its nearest neighbours are Greenland (287km/178 miles), the Faroe Islands (420km/261 miles), Scotland (798km/496 miles) and Norway (970km/603 miles). Given those distances, Iceland is clearly part of Europe.

The country covers an area of 103,000 sq. km (39,768 sq. miles), but only 20 percent of this area is available for use (including grassland). The rest is barren waste (54 percent), glacier (12 percent), lava (11 percent) or inland waters (3 percent). The longest river in Iceland is the Þjórsá (230km/143 miles); the largest natural lake, fiingvallavatn (83 sq km/32 sq miles); the largest inland lake, fiórisvatn (which serves as a reservoir for the hydro-electric power station on the Þjórsá); the highest waterfall, Glymur (190m/623ft; at the end of Hvalfjörður); the highest mountain, Hvannadalshnúkur (2,119m/

6,952ft); the largest ice-cap, Vatnajökull (8,400 sq. km/3,242 sq. miles); the largest island, Heimaey (13.4 sq. km/5.17 sq. miles).

POPULATION

With only 2.8 people per sq. km, the total population of Iceland is about 299,000 – roughly the same as a smaller British city such as Plymouth – which makes it one of the most sparsely populated countries in Europe. Around four percent of the population are not native Icelanders (with most migrants coming from eastern Europe and Scadinavian countries). At 83 for women, and 78 for men, life expectancy is well above the European average.

Below: City Hall, Reykjavík
Bottom: DJ Jo Lively hits the decks in Reykjavík

Around 60 percent of the population live in the metropolitan area of Reykjavík. Five of the 10 largest towns in the country are part of this conurbation. They are: Reykjavík (pop. 115,000), Kópavogur (pop. 26,500), Hafnarfjörður (pop. 22,500), Garðabær (pop. 9,500) and Mossfellsbær (pop. 6,500).

The largest towns outside this region are Akureyri (just under 17,000), Reykjanesbær (Keflavík and neighbouring towns; pop. 11,400), Akranes (pop. 6,000), Heimaey (Westman Islands; pop. 4,500).

CLIMATE AND WHEN TO GO

Iceland lies just south of the Arctic Circle, but the warm air from the Gulf Stream contributes to relatively settled weather patterns and, for these latitudes, mild temperatures. Winters are often severe with lots of rainfall, but an examination of the statistics reveals that Icelandic winters are no colder than those in much of northern continental Europe. Summers are cool with average temperatures in the region of 10°C (50°F).

Daytime temperatures of over 20°C (68°F) can be enjoyed in sheltered spots inland, more rarely in the coastal regions. In the central highlands night frosts are likely to occur throughout the year, in other parts of the country between the months of September and May. Rainfall is highest on the southern slopes of the glaciers. The regions north of Vatnajökull generally have less rainfall. A characteristic feature of the island is rapid weather and wind changes. Visitors to Iceland are often reminded of the old saying: 'If you don't like the weather, then just wait five minutes'.

THE MIDNIGHT SUN

Because the earth is tilted, the polar regions constantly face the sun at their respective summer solstices and face away from it in the winter. The Arctic and Antarctic circles at 66.5° north and south latitude respectively are the southern and northern limits of constant daylight on the longest day of the year.

While the offshore island of Grímsey straddles the Arctic Circle, the rest of Iceland lies to the south of the line. The northern town of Akureyri is about 100km (60 miles) away. Although the sun does partially set on the summer solstice, Akureyri enjoys very light evenings and it likes to describe itself as the 'town of the midnight sun'.

FLORA AND FAUNA

Iceland's range of flora is a function of the country's position just south of the Arctic Circle.

When to Visit
The best time to visit Iceland is during the months of July and August. Evenings stay light from the middle of May to the end of August. At other times of the year the chances of seeing the Northern Lights are reasonably good as long as the nights are clear of cloud. Iceland does not experience polar nights, i.e. days without sunlight. The months of February, March and April are best for winter tours.

Midnight sun

Grassland dominates on the meadows, moorland and heaths. About 500 types of more advanced plants have been recorded, but mosses and lichens also abound. Because of Iceland's isolated position, little plant immigration has taken place. The harsh climate and human influences, such as deforestation in the Middle Ages and overgrazing, have restricted the spread of plant life.

Apart from insects and fish, Icelandic fauna means almost exclusively birds. There are some 80 different species of breeding birds. About three dozen-plus species of migratory birds have been recorded as regular visitors to the island, and another 200 species have been sighted. Maritime and wading birds make up the largest groups. The arctic fox is the only native mammal; others, such as the mink, rat and reindeer, have been brought here by human beings.

Iceland's Time Zone
Iceland lies well to the west of the European mainland, but it stays in touch with European business time by using Greenwich Mean Time, even though the clocks should, according to the International Time Zone, be at least one hour, in western Iceland two hours, behind. Consequently, on the night of 21–22 June, the sun sets relatively late – after 1am – and then only for about 20 minutes.

THE PEOPLE

The Icelandic people are pragmatists. Their way of life may appear chaotic at times, but in fact they have a remarkable talent for organisation – many a tourist can tell a tale about that. They will not impose themselves upon their guests and it is not in their nature to be too familiar with strangers. In fact, they may come over as rather uncommunicative, but this does not mean that

Puffin: national symbol

they reject outsiders. It is simply a sign of their cautious nature, more evident in the countryside than in the town. Another characteristic is the Icelandic people's habit of not saying directly what they want, but to use circumlocutions to indicate what they don't want – but then that is just being sensitive to others.

There are, of course, many differences among the almost 300,000 inhabitants. The young people who live in the capital, for example, grow up with very open-minded attitudes. As well as speaking Icelandic, almost everyone speaks near-perfect English. Fashion trends from both sides of the Atlantic are quickly adopted. International culture, kept at bay for centuries due to Iceland's isolation, is now rapidly absorbed through satellite dishes, the internet and CDs.

Formal moral codes are alien to Icelanders. A third of all children are born outside marriage, but two-thirds of such children live with parents who are in long-term, stable partnerships, generally equal in status to that of a legal marriage. About every tenth child grows up in a single-parent family.

Family names are used only in exceptional cases. The general rule is that a new addition to the family is given a first name and a surname, comprising the first name of the father – seldom that of the mother – and the ending 'son' for son or 'dóttir' for daughter. Ásdís Magnúsdóttir and Guðmundur Gíslason, together with daughter Björk Guðmundsdóttir and son Grettir Guðmundsson, would constitute a typical Icelandic family. The surname is not usually used as a form of address. No one would say 'Hello, Ólafur Ragnar, son of Grímur', even if the person in question is the country's president. 'Hello, Ólafur', or in certain circumstances 'Hello, President Ólafur', would be the correct form of address.

Below: sushi chef
Bottom: friendly local

RELIGION

More than 90 percent of the population belong to the Evangelical Lutheran church and three percent to other Protestant denominations.

Roman Catholics and believers in ancient Germanic gods count for less than one percent each.

LANGUAGE

Icelanders born in the 20th century are still able to read the literature of forebears born in the 12th and 13th centuries in the original language. This is because, unlike other European languages, their mother tongue has changed little since the Middle Ages. Outsiders generally find it very difficult to get to grips with the Icelandic language because of some very complicated grammatical rules and unusual pronunciation. The only thing that is easy to grasp is the rule about emphasis. It is always the first syllable which is stressed. The many accents on letters have nothing to do with emphasis. The everyday language for tourists is always English.

ECONOMY

Fish has been the main impetus in the development of Iceland's economy. Two-thirds of the country's exports are fish products. For years, there have been problems arising from the overfishing of the waters around Iceland. Strict quotas will, it is hoped, lead to an improvement in fish stocks, but these restrictions have been respon-

Linguistic Purity
Icelanders believe it is important to keep the Icelandic language free of foreign influences. The English neologisms that have entered so many other languages have no place in Icelandic. Where necessary, new words are created. A fax, for example, is simply a *'bréfasími'*, or a 'letter telephone'. The word *'sími'* for telephone is derived from an old word meaning 'wire'.

Trendy shopping on Laugavegur, Reykjavík

sible for many job losses. The unemployment rate, for decades an insignificant figure, has been fluctuating over recent years but currently stands at around 2 percent. Tourism is the second most important sector in Iceland's economy, welcoming around 400,000 visitors every year, with British and Germans the largest groups.

The heavily subsidised agricultural sector mainly supplies the domestic market. As a consequence of the drive to reduce soil erosion after freely grazing sheep reduced the sparse vegetation, flocks have been cut from almost 800,000 at the end of the 1980s to roughly half that figure.

Industrial development on an island that has few raw materials has been modest. But, given the cheap sources of power on the island, Iceland has become a desirable location for energy-intensive manufacturing processes, such as aluminium smelting. Other major exports are equipment for the fishing industry and software for various industries.

Below: fishing crates
Bottom: catch of the day

WHALING

In 1985 Iceland ended commercial whaling, but allowed 'scientific' whaling to continue until 1989. At the time the country was open to criticism from Greenpeace. Iceland was also pilloried at international level, but no one tried to change the attitude of the Icelanders themselves by lending support to opponents of whaling there.

There is a long tradition of protecting whales in Iceland. In 1915 whaling was banned in Icelandic waters and this ruling lasted for 10 years. Iceland has never been one of the great whaling nations. In economic terms, the hunting of these giants of the sea has always been of little value. On the other hand, international calls for a boycott of Icelandic products had catastrophic consequences for the countries' fish exports. Iceland's insistence on its right to continue whaling can be seen as the protest of a small nation fed up with being bullied by the superpowers.

In 1992 Iceland left the International Whaling Commission and, together with other North

Atlantic nations, founded NAMMCO (North Atlantic Marine Mammal Commission). This body aims to preserve the whale, but also to allow whaling as long as it can be proved scientifically that whale stocks are not threatened.

In 1989 Iceland finally bowed to international pressure and banned commercial whaling. However, domestic opinion remained stubbornly in favour of whaling and in August 2003 scientific whaling was resumed. This is seen as a first step towards recommencing commercial whaling within the jurisdiction of the international whaling commission (which Iceland rejoined in 2002).

Below: whaling ships in Reykjavík harbour
Bottom: Icelandic Parliament

POLITICS

Under the constitution, the Icelandic parliament, the Alþing, must be re-elected every four years, but circumstances often force elections to be brought forward. Coalition governments are the rule rather than the exception.

Standing above the political fray is a directly elected president. Between 1980 and 1996, this was the non-political Vigdís Finnbogadóttir. Her successor, the socialist and professional politician, Ólafur Ragnar Grímsson, would have lost against Finnbogadóttir, a popular ex-theatre director, had she decided to seek a fifth term.

Iceland is well represented in international organisations. It is a member of NATO, although it has no military forces of its own. But membership of economic groupings has always been a problem. Until a few years ago entry into the European Union (EU) would have been inconceivable, given the fisheries policies adopted in Brussels. The political parties now adopt differing views on the issue. Iceland is currently part of the European Economic Area, an extension of the European Union, and enjoys the same status as Norway.

For historical reasons, Iceland has always maintained close links with the countries of northern Europe and is a member of the Nordic Council. Iceland, Greenland and the Faroe Islands make up a West Nordic region within which there are special economic and cultural links.

THE SAGAS

The first permanent settlement on Iceland dates from 874, when Ingólfur Arnarson landed on the island. Two other journeys to the island before then are known about. One expedition for settlers ended in failure and a group of Irish monks lived on the island until the 9th century. This information is recorded in two unique medieval volumes: the *Íslendingabók* by Ari fiorgilsson, a summary of the history of Iceland from 874 to 1120, and the *Landnámabók* (Book of Settlements) by an unknown writer. This lists about 400 important settlement treks with the name of the leader.

During the 11th and 12th centuries, some 40 Icelandic sagas were recorded. In medieval times, these epic tales were highly regarded throughout Europe. Written in prose, some were based on oral traditions, most were works by unknown authors. The sagas look back over one to two centuries and describe events – often true – about important characters or clans in Iceland between 930 and 1030, a period known as the Saga Age. At the same time they served as propaganda, boosting the reputation of the island's elite.

Voyages of Discovery
The sagas possess a degree of authenticity not just with regard to the figures who feature in them, but also with regard to the customs and way of life at that time. As historical sources they continue to be of only limited value, although they did gain added authority when the Norwegian archaeologist, Helge Ingstad, used two of them to locate a Viking settlement on Canada's east coast. Excavations proved that Norsemen discovered America 500 years before Christopher Columbus... and you can read about it in the Greenland Saga and the Saga of Eric the Red. For centuries, nobody took the stories seriously.

Young Icelander

HISTORICAL HIGHLIGHTS

AD225–305 Roman coins dating from this time found in southern and eastern Iceland. Historians are uncertain about their origin. Were Roman soldiers, perhaps blown off course, the first Europeans to land on Iceland or did later settlers bring the coins with them?

7th century Irish monks and the first Norse settlers arrive in Iceland.

793 The attack on the monastery at Lindisfarne off the coast of Northumberland in England marks the beginning of the Viking era.

874 Ingólfur Arnason, the 'First Settler', lands in a bay on the southwest coast, near the site of modern Reykjavík. Over the next decades, more settlers follow. Most of the new arrivals come from western Norway. About one in 10 originate from Norse settlements on the Scottish islands and Ireland. This immigration can be partly attributed to a Norwegian king to whom many clan leaders and landowners were unwilling to submit.

930 End of the 'Age of Settlement': Iceland's population is now about 25,000. All available land is divided up. The Icelandic Parliament, the Alþing, is founded. Beginning of the Saga Age (until 1030).

1000 Discovery of North America by Leifur Eiríksson. Christianity is adopted as Iceland's official religion. The first bishopric is established in Skálholt in 1056.

1179 Birth of Snorri Sturluson, historian, diplomat and saga writer.

1241 Murder of Snorri Sturluson, by order of the King of Norway.

1262 Voluntary submission to the Norwegian crown, which from 1380 onwards rests on the heads of Danish monarchs. 16th century Hanseatic trading posts founded, e.g. in Hafnarfjörður *(see page 25)*.

1541 Reformation in southern Iceland and in 1550 in northern Iceland.

1602 Introduction of Danish trade monopoly, prohibiting Iceland from trading with any other countries. It remains in Danish hands until 1854.

1783–85 Eruption of the Laki crater *(see page 69)* decimates the population. The Danes consider resettling the 40,000 or so surviving Icelanders in Denmark.

1800 Abolition of the Althing on orders of the Danish king.

1814 At the end of the Napoleonic Wars Denmark loses Norway to archrivals Sweden, but retains power over the old Norwegian possessions of Iceland, Greenland and the Faroe Islands.

1843 Independence movement under Jón Sigurðsson (1811–79) brings about the re-instatement of the Alﬂing.

1874 To celebrate the 1,000th anniversary of settlement of the island, Christian IX visits Iceland, the first Danish monarch to do so. He brings with him a new constitution, which from 1904 gives Iceland far-reaching autonomy in internal affairs.

1915 Iceland gets its own flag. Introduction of female suffrage for parliamentary elections.

1918 Union agreement with Denmark. The Danish king continues to be head of state, but the country is independent in every other respect.

1940 To protect Iceland from German occupation during World War II, British troops land on Iceland. Under a defence agreement, they are replaced in 1941 by Americans. Iceland is of great strategic importance in keeping Allied forces in the North Atlantic supplied.

1944 Iceland unilaterally withdraws from the union agreement with Denmark and becomes a republic on 17 June (National Independence Day).

1946 Iceland joins the United Nations. Start of commercial whaling.

1949 Iceland abandons its neutrality and becomes a member of NATO.

1952 Extension of the fishery protection zone to 4 nautical miles. As with all subsequent extensions (1958 to 12 miles/ 19km, 1972 to 50 miles/80km, 1976 to 200 miles/320km), the decision is opposed by other fishing nations, mainly Great Britain (the Cod Wars).

1963 The volcanic island of Surtsey emerges from the sea southwest of the Westman Islands.

1973 Volcanic eruption forces the evacuation of Heimaey Island's 5,000 inhabitants. The harbour is saved by volunteers who manage to divert the lava flow.

1976 A 200-mile fishing limit off the coast of Iceland is agreed.

1980 Vigdís Finnbogadóttir becomes president of Iceland. She is re-elected three times, and holds office until 1996.

From 1984 Fishing quotas introduced to protect fish stocks in Icelandic waters.

1985 Iceland ends commercial whaling. The controversial practice of 'scientific' whaling continues until 1989.

1986 Presidents Gorbachev and Reagan arrive in Reykjavík for a summit on ending the Cold War.

1992 Iceland leaves International Whaling Commission after rejection of request for limited whaling quota. Subsequently stops whaling, but does not declare itself a non-whaling country.

1994 Iceland enters the EEA.

1996 A volcano under Vatnajökull erupts. A month later, meltwater and ice floes as big as houses break out from under the ice (glacier burst) and wash 8km (5 miles) of Iceland's Ring Road into the sea. Ólafur Ragnar Grímsson becomes president.

2000 Iceland celebrates one thousand years of Christianity and Leifur Eiríksson's discovery of North America in the year 1000. Reykjavík is voted a European City of Culture. Mount Helka erupts on and new lava stretches 3–4 km (2–3 miles). Several earthquakes hit the south of the island in June.

2002 Iceland joins the International Whaling Commission.

2003 Iceland resumes 'scientific whaling' amid international environmental outcry. The government decides to build a vast dam in the highland wilderness at Kárhnjúkar to power a US-owned aluminium smelter in the East Fjords.

2006 Without a regular army or armed police, the government creates an 80-strong paramilitary Icelandic Crisis Response Unit. Their first controversial posting is to Afghanistan. US forces withdraw from the Keflavík military base, ending a 65 year presence and almost 1,000 local jobs in the area.

2007 Icelandic population predicted to pass the 300,000 mark.

Map
below

👁 Clean air

However appropriate it may have seemed to Ingólfur, the name 'Smoky Bay' is now a long way from the truth. Apart from motor vehicle exhausts, Reykjavik is effectively a smoke-free zone. All of the houses are heated with geothermal energy. From the numerous vantage points around the city, the air above the colourful roofs of this modern, spacious capital always looks fresh and clear.

Preceding pages: Gullfoss
Below: View of
Reykjavík's rooftops

1: Reykjavík

As he approached Iceland for the first time, Ingólfur Arnarson, the country's first permanent settler, tossed his high-seat pillars overboard, so that the gods could direct them to the settlement that they had chosen for him. The tree trunks, ornate with carvings, eventually found their way to a large bay in the southwest of Iceland, where steam from hot springs rose up into the air. Ingólfur

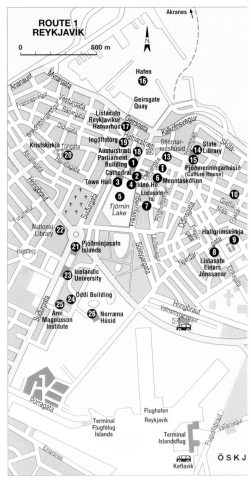

called his new home 'Smoky Bay' or Reykjavík. In 1786 a town that had barely 200 inhabitants won its municipal charter. The centre of the city now has 115,000 inhabitants, and almost 70,000 people live in the suburbs.

The following two circular tours capture the atmosphere of the Icelandic capital and cover the main places of interest, and can easily be completed on foot. For the third tour, however, some form of transport is recommended.

Map
on pages
22–3

Light Nights

Iðnó is the setting for one of Reykjavík's most popular tourist shows, Light Nights; the drama is based on the sagas and Viking tales and is performed every Sunday and Monday in summer at 8.30pm. The building also houses a quaint coffee bar and an excellent restaurant.

A TOUR THROUGH THE CITY CENTRE

To obtain a good first impression of the city, start this circular tour at the tourist office at Aðalstræti 2, where up-to-date information is available. Overlooking Austurvöllur Square is the **Parliament Building ❶**, the Alþing, the oldest parliament in the world. After centuries in Þingvellir (*see page 38*), it was moved to Reykjavík in 1845 and then installed in its present premises in 1881, when the island was still under Danish rule, as illustrated by the royal coat-of-arms of Christian IX above the doorway.

In the middle of Austurvöllur stands a statue of the father of independent Iceland, Jón Sigurðsson (*see page 87*). A font in front of the altar of the rather plain **Cathedral ❷**, situated on the east side of the square, is the work of Bertel Thorvaldsen. The Dane with an Icelandic father was one of the most important sculptors of the 19th-century neoclassical era.

THE TOWN HALL

The Icelandic parliament building looks small when compared to the bold **Town Hall ❸**, which was completed in 1992. Because of the shortage of space in the central area, it was built over the water on the northern shore of Tjörnin Lake. The

Tjörnin Lake

spiralling costs for this building were a source of controversy at the time. A large relief map of Iceland can be viewed inside.

A footbridge links the Town Hall with ★ **Iðnó House** ❹, a beautifully restored timber construction dating from the late 19th century. It is now a popular cultural centre and theatre.

Tjörnin Lake ❺, a peaceful haven in the heart of the city, is well known for its rich bird life. From the northeast corner **Menntaskólinn** ❻, the long-established grammar school, is visible above Lækjargata. Before 1847 it was the only school in the country that offered pupils a route to university, usually one in Denmark.

THE NATIONAL GALLERY

★★ **Listasafn Íslands** ❼, the National Gallery of Iceland (Fríkirkjuvegur 7), is set in the architecturally effective combination of an old ice warehouse and a light and airy, modern structure. It is used primarily for temporary exhibitions of modern and contemporary Icelandic art. Visitors may well be tempted by the café on the first floor (Tuesday–Sunday 11am–5pm).

Directly in front of it is **Listasafn Einars Jónssonar** ❽ (Eiríksgata), a museum in the former home and studio of the sculptor Einar Jónsson (1874–1954). A cross-section of his work, much of which depicts mythological and religious symbolism, is in the sculpture garden behind (February–November daily 2–5pm; closed Monday, June–September; entrance fee).

HALLGRIMSKIRKJA

The ★★ **Hallgrímskirkja** ❾ was designed by Guðjón Samúelsson (1887–1950), for many years the national architect. Dominating the city centre, it can be seen from many miles away. It was finally consecrated in 1987 after a 40-year construction period. The exterior, considered by some to be extremely ugly, is reminiscent of Icelandic basalt rock formations, while the airy interior with its tall, slender concrete columns has a distinctive

Star Attractions
- Hallgrímskirkja
- Listasafn Íslands

Exterior (below) and interior (bottom) of Hallgrímskirkja

Map
on pages
22–3

The great auk

The city's Natural History Museum has a specimen of the extinct great auk. Related to guillemots, razorbills and puffins, the great auk once lived in huge colonies in Iceland, North America, Greenland and the Faeroes. These flightless birds, standing around 70cm (30 inches) high, were easy prey for hunters and their numbers gradually declined in the 19th century. The last surviving pair was killed on Eldey island, southwest of the Rejkjanes peninsula, in 1844.

Gothic look. Equipped with an enormous ★ 72-register German organ and 5,275 pipes, the Hallgrímskirkja is noted for its fine acoustics. The highlight of the church, however, is the 75-m (245-ft) high platform in the tower, which offers the best possible view over Reykjavík (viewing platform: daily 10am–5pm).

LAUGAVEGUR

Several routes lead from the church to **Laugavegur ⑩**, a busy shopping street. Geothermal underfloor heating keeps the pavements free of snow and ice during the winter. The international designer fashion shops in Laugavegur, Bankastræti and Hverfisgata offer particularly good value as a 15 percent VAT reduction is available to foreign visitors *(see page 116)*. The same applies to the elegant jewellery and superior-quality clocks and watches.

SOLFAR SUNCRAFT

Take a detour from here to see the **Sólfar Suncraft ⑪** on the banks of the Viðeyjarsund. This modern work of art made of stainless steel by Gunnar Árnason (1931–89) was built in 1986. Come and enjoy Iceland's romantic sunsets at this waterside spot. Follow the road to the east and

Sólfar Suncraft

you come to Hlemmur Square and the ★★ **Náttúr-ufræðistofnun Íslands** , Iceland's Natural History Museum, which is full of fascinating exhibits on the country's geology and flora and fauna (Tuesday, Thursday, Saturday, Sunday: summer 1–5pm; winter 1.30–4.30pm).

Star Attraction
● **Natural History Museum**

THE UNIVERSITY QUARTER

Opposite Lækjartorg square at the junction of Lækjargata and Bankastræti, stands the **Stjórnarráðshúsið** ⓭, built during the colonial era as a prison but now used as the offices of the Icelandic prime minister.

Make the short detour to the north to Arnarhóll and the **monument to Ingólfur Arnarson**, Iceland's first settler, then take a few steps into Hverfisgata to the building where the **State Library** ⓮ was housed and which is now an art and cultural centre. Close by, the **Þjóðmen-ningarhúsið** ⓯ contains a first-class exhibition of medieval manuscripts, Iceland's famous Sagas and Eddas, the country's most treasured ancient relics (daily 11am–5pm).

Below and bottom: whale-watching ships and shipping reels in Rekjavík harbour

THE HARBOUR

Many cruise ships call in at Reykjavík and they moor in the **hafen** (harbour) ⓰. Directly opposite the quay, in the Tollhúsið (Tryggvagata 19), you may find a bargain at the ★ **Kolaportið Flea Market** (Saturday and Sunday 11am–5pm). The food section is a good opportunity to sample some typical Icelandic delicacies such as cured shark and pickled rams' testicles.

At Tryggvagata 17 is **Listasafn Reykjavíkur Hafnarhús** ⓱, the Reykjavik Art Museum (daily 10am–5pm). Follow the traffic-calmed **Aus-turstræti** ⓲ shopping street to the modern **Ingólfstorg** ⓳, built in 1994. This is often the venue on Sundays for cultural events. Later in the evening it becomes a lively meeting place for skaters and motorcyclists.

Carved falcons on the roof ridges of the Falcon House on the north side of the Ingólfstorg

Map on pages 22–3

The Sagas
The Árni Magnússon Institute contains precious manuscripts that were returned to Iceland from Denmark between 1971 and 1997. They had been there since Magnússon (1663–1730), an Icelandic scholar who collected historical documents relating to his country, bequeathed his collection to the University of Copenhagen. Icelanders have a great respect for their cultural heritage: the sagas are standard texts in schools and are still read for pleasure in their original form, since the written language has changed little since the Middle Ages.

serve as a reminder of this building's original function. During the colonial era gerfalcons from all over the country were collected here before being presented to the European aristocracy as gifts from the Danish king. There is plenty of activity during weekend evenings as Icelanders trawl by car or on foot along Laugavegur to Ingólfstorg between restaurants and bars. Built in 1764, it was once the home of Bishop Geir Víðalín, whose generous hospitality eventually earned him the dubious distinction of being the only bishop in history to be declared bankrupt.

KRISTSKIRKJA

Túngata climbs up hill to the Catholic **Kristskirkja ㉕**. Before the Hallgrímskirkja was completed, this was the largest church in the city, even though only 1 percent of Icelanders are Catholics.

On the way to the university quarter you will see the ★ **Þjóðminjasafn Íslands ㉑** (Suðurgata 41), the National Museum, essential viewing for anyone interested in Icelandic history and contemporary society. Exhibits include art, handicrafts and tools dating from the Viking era (May–August, Tuesday–Sunday 10am–5pm; September–April, Tuesday–Sunday 11am–5pm; entrance fee).

The National Museum

THE NATIONAL LIBRARY AND UNIVERSITY

On the other side of the road stands a distinctive, modern building, known to the locals as the 'book castle'. Iceland's **National Library** ㉒ does indeed look like a fortified building. Housed under one roof are both the National Library and the University Library.

The **Icelandic University** (Háskóli Íslands) ㉓ moved into the main block in 1940. Now this seat of learning with nine faculties has just over 9,000 students. To find out what life is like in an Icelandic University, enter the **Oddi Building** ㉔ and view the university's art collection in the corridor. The full collection of world-famous saga manuscripts is kept under carefully controlled conditions in the ★ **Árni Magnússon Institute** ㉕, another university building, but only those on public display in the Culture House (Þjóðmenningarhúsið) are available for inspection.

THE EXHIBITION CENTRE

On your way back to the city centre, stop for a refreshment break at the cafeteria in the **Norræna Húsið** ㉖. This cultural exhibition centre, opened in 1968, was a gift from the Scandinavian nations for the promotion of cultural exchanges. It is just one of the fine public buildings designed by the renowned Finnish architect, Alvar Aalto.

POOLS AND GARDENS

This circular tour can be completed on foot, but it passes through some suburban areas and industrial zones where there is little of interest. Rather than walk the whole way, a bicycle or a car would be more suitable. Start out from Hlemmur Square by the **Natural History Museum** *(see page 27)*. Students of modern history will be familiar with the role played by the **Höfði House** ㉗. It was here in 1986 where Mikhail Gorbachev and Ronald Reagan met for their first superpower summit – which marked the beginning of the end of the Cold War.

The **Sigurjón Ólafsson Museum** ㉘ (Laugarnestangi 70) pays homage to the painter and

Below: Hofði
Bottom: Norræna Húsið

Map on pages 22–3

Beware the hot tub
When visiting Sundlaugar Reykjavíkur swimming pool, do take the chance to relax in one of the geothermal hot tubs, but don't make the mistake of jumping into the emptiest one: it will almost certainly be the hottest, at around 45°C (113°F). Start in the coolest pot, which will be about 37°C (98°F).

sculptor Sigurjón Ólafsson (1908–82). Mainly he used materials that the sea deposited outside his studio and which he then collected as he strolled along the shoreline. The museum is situated by the sea and the view from the museum across his sculptures by the shore and sweeping out over the Atlantic is stunning.

MONASTIC ISLAND

A boat leaves regularly from a jetty in the commercial **Sundahöfn harbour** ❷ to the island of ★ **Viðey**. Only a few overgrown remains from the herb garden have survived from the medieval Augustinian monastery, but **Viðeyarstofa House** is Iceland's oldest stone building. It was restored in the 1980s and now houses a **gourmet restaurant** (tel: 568 1045). On the west side of the island a circular walk takes in a piece of landscape art by Richard Serra, known as Áfangar.

Ásmundarsafn

THE CITY'S LARGEST SWIMMING POOL

No one should leave Reykjavík without visiting one of the swimming pools. The city's largest pool is ★ **Sundlaugar Reykjavíkur** ❸ (Sundlaugarvegur; Monday–Friday 6am–9.30pm, Saturday and Sunday 8am–8pm). It is situated to the east of the city centre in Laugardalur.

THE BOTANICAL GARDENS

Further up in **Laugardalur** ❸, the **Botanical Gardens** give a detailed and informative background to Iceland's flora. Children will appreciate the adjoining **zoo**. Most of the animals are domesticated, but there are birds, seals and reindeer. There is also a **playground** for children.

On the way back to the city there is another opportunity to absorb Icelandic art and culture. ★ **Ásmundarsafn** ❸ (Sigtún 5; May–September, daily 10am–4pm; October–April, 1–4pm; the sculpture park is always open) is a museum dedicated to the work of Ásmundur Sveinsson, without doubt Iceland's most famous sculptor.

THE SUBURBS

★★ **Árbæjarsafn** ㉝ in the suburb of Árbær is an open-air museum with a collection of mainly rural, but also urban buildings from the past two centuries. They are often used as settings for demonstrations of old craft skills (June–August, Tuesday–Friday 10am–5pm, Saturday and Sunday 10am–6pm; open by arrangement in winter, tel: 577 1111, www.arbaejarsafn.is; bus 19 from the city centre).

Kjarvalsstaðir ㉞ (Flókagata 9; daily 10am–5pm), the municipal art museum, has a wide collection by Iceland's most famous painter, Jóhannes S. Kjarval (1885–1972). Temporary exhibitions are also held alongside.

Kringlan ㉟, a super-modern shopping arcade, is the centre of a purpose-built complex. As well as small shops and supermarkets, this is where visitors will find one of the legendary Hard Rock cafés. On view are rock memorabilia. On sale are Hard Rock T-shirts and sweatshirts.

PERLAN

The heating and hot water for the city of Reykjavík used to be collected in five huge tanks on **Öskjuhlíð Hill** ㊱ on the eastern edge of the city airport. Mounted on the tanks is ★ **Perlan** (The Pearl), a glass dome visible from miles away with

Star Attraction •
Árbæjarsafn

Below: Kjarvalsstaðir
Bottom: Reykjavík zoo

Map on pages 22–3

Below: Perlan
Bottom: Hafnarfjörður's oldest house

access to a viewing platform, and magnificent views. On the ground floor, the **Saga Museum** (summer daily 10am–6pm, winter weekdays only noon–5pm; entrance fee) is Iceland's answer to London's Madame Tussaud's with life-like wax models of characters from the Viking age.

OUTSIDE THE CITY

Look out to the southwest from any of the vantage points in Reykjavík and you are bound to see a free-standing, gleaming white building. **Bessastaðir** on the **Álftanes** promontory is the residence of the head of state. Since the Middle Ages this has been the home of Iceland's most powerful and important figures. One resident was Snorri Sturluson, the Edda author.

SOUTHERN NEIGHBOUR

★ **Hafnarfjörður**, Reykjavík's neighbour to the south, has not been overwhelmed by the capital's suburbs and has managed to retain its independence. The centre of the town lies beside the fine natural harbour, which made the place very attractive to merchants from northern Germany during the period of Hanseatic trade.

Situated by the harbour now is the ★ **Hafnarfjörður Museum** (June–August, daily 1–5pm; September–May, Saturday and Sunday 1–5pm) containing an overview of the town's history in photographs and other exhibits. Next door (same times), **Sívertsens-Húsið**, is the oldest building in town, now restored to its original state.

The two buildings and the romantic **Restaurant A. Hansen** (Vesturgata 4; tel: 565 1130) make an attractive ensemble of 19th-century houses. **Hafnarborg** (Strandgata 34) is an artistic and cultural centre often used for exhibitions (Wednesday–Monday 11am–5pm).

At some time visitors to the town should take a trip round the **Hellisgerði** lava park, a green area in a bizarre tract of lava, which can easily be imagined as the home of elves and trolls. Hafnarfjörður likes to describe itself as the capital of their kingdom.

REYKANES

Suðurnes, Iceland's southwestern peninsula, often known as **Reykjanes**, is the site of Keflavík international airport, the gateway to Iceland. This is the part of the country that most newly arriving visitors see first and many of them get quite a shock, because the journey from Keflavík to Reykjavík passes through some particularly barren countryside. But this is not the whole story, for this peninsula does also have some spectacular coastline, mainly to the south and southwest. The area is especially popular with birdwatchers at migration time.

THE BLUE LAGOON

★★ **Bláa Lonið** (Blue Lagoon), to the north of the fishing village of Grindavík, is one of Iceland's principal attractions. In 1999 the bathing facilities were moved to a new and extravagantly designed site in the heart of a bizarre lava field. The pool is fed by a constant supply of warm water (40°C/104°F) rich in silica, salt and other elements. The salty water emerges from a borehole 1,500m (5,000ft) deep. Only after the water has passed through a heat exchanger and supplied energy to a power station and a heating system is it cool enough for bathers. For details, tel: 420 8800; fax: 420 8801; www.bluelagoon.com.

Star Attraction
● **Blue Lagoon**

Healing waters
Relaxing in the Blue Lagoon is said to be beneficial for mind and body, particularly the skin. The on-site clinic at the Blue Lagoon uses the special healing powers of the water as a successful treatment for psoriasis. For those who just wish to pamper themselves, there is a range of massage and body treatments, a sauna and a steam bath in a lava cave. This is sure to work up an appetite, so visit the modern restaurant with its huge glass window overlooking the Lagoon.

Bathing at the Bláa Lonið

Map
on page
35

2: Around Reyjkavík

Reykjavík – Gullfoss – Stóri-Geysir – Þingvellir – Reykjavík (250km/155 miles)

This route is the '**Golden Circle**', the classic tour for new arrivals. It takes in the greenhouse capital of Hveragerði, the Kerið explosion crater, Gullfoss 'Golden Waterfall' and the hot springs in Haukadalur with the active Strokkur geyser. There is nowhere better to get a feel for Iceland's history than Þingvellir National Park, where the Icelandic parliament, the Alþing, first assembled over 1,000 years ago. The route can be completed within one day. Without the detour to Stöng, it will take 8–9 hours; otherwise allow 10 to 12 hours.

Below: Hekla
Bottom: Þjórsárdalur

SKIING AREAS

Set out from **Reykjavík** *(see page 22)* along the southbound Ring Road. Bláfjöll to the south of the Ring Road and Hengill to the north both provide good skiing with downhills and cross-country tracks. The best time for skiing are the months of February and March.

When you reach the eastern end of the barren **Hellisheiði** plain, the view over Iceland's southern coast opens up and, on a clear day, it is possible to see as far as the Westman Islands. Down below is the greenhouse town of **Hveragerði** (38km/24 miles; *see Route 5 page 73)*.

Just before Selfoss leave the Ring Road and follow Highway 35 towards Gullfoss and Geysir.

SKALHOLT

The explosion crater of ★ **Kerið** (61km/38 miles) is a fine example of what geologists call a maar, i.e. a shallow, flat-floored crater probably formed by multiple explosive eruptions. This one – the finest of its kind in Iceland – is some 55m (180ft) deep and shaped like an amphitheatre.

Skálholt (85km/53 miles) was for a long time the spiritual capital of Iceland. From 1056 until the Reformation, which reached southern Iceland in 1541, it was the seat of 32 Catholic bishops. A counter-Reformation movement ended in 1550 with the beheading of the last Catholic bishop of northern Iceland, Jón Arason *(see page 46)*. A memorial stone here recalls this event.

Skálholt saw a further 13 Protestant bishops before an earthquake badly damaged the cathedral and the theological school, forcing the church dignitaries to move to Reykjavík.

HEKLA

Soon after you reach Highway 30, Highway 32 forks off to **Þjórsárdalur**. This road offers stunning views over the Þjórsá river and towards one of the best-known and most active central volcanoes in Iceland, the 1,491-m (4,891-ft) high ★ **Hekla**. The last eruption from its 5-km (3-mile) long volcanic fissure occurred in 2000 and lasted 11 days. Further eruptions could take place at any time.

Many earlier visitors from the European mainland described Hekla as the 'gateway to hell', from where the cries of sinners could be heard. Instead of burning in hell, why not unwind in the warm water of the nearby **Þjórsárdalslaug** thermal bath (turn off after 30km/19 miles) while enjoying the magnificent mountain panorama.

Eleventh church
The present church at Skálholt (1956–63) is the eleventh to be built here. All its predecessors were of timber.

Icelandic horse

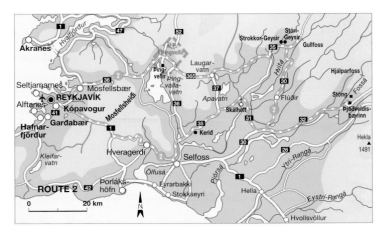

Map on page 35

The geyser awakes

For years the Great Geyser was inactive and attempts were made to bring it back to life by pouring soap flakes down the tube. This, however, was deemed to be environmentally unacceptable, and in the end nature took its own course: in 2000 an earthquake awoke Great Geyser from its slumber and now once again columns of hot water shoot 60m (200ft) into the air.

HJALPARFOSS

To reach the spectacular ★ **Hjálparfoss** falls, which are decorated with basalt columns and split in two by a rock, take the short track that branches off near the bridge over the Fossá river (the turning is 30km/19 miles from Highway 32, open only in summer) and then follow the west bank of the river southwards for a few hundred metres.

VIKING HOUSE

Þjóðveldisbærinn, a reconstruction of a Viking house, was built in 1974 to mark the 1,100th anniversary of the Settlement. The main room with a central fireplace was used as a workroom and communal dormitory. Only the farm owner and his wife enjoyed some privacy in the alcove along one side. Two annexes, each with one room, led off the main hall. One was the 'best room' where the women would sit spinning and weaving and where celebrations were held, the other was for the dairy cows and the preparation and storage of butter and milk.

You may be surprised by the size of the toilet opposite the entrance: during the Viking period 'spending a penny' was a collective activity.

Just before you reach the reconstruction, a rough track runs up to the north to the original building. **Stöng** farmhouse was buried under

Thundering Gullfoss

ash after Hekla erupted in 1104. Archaeologists uncovered the site in 1939, with medieval saga texts assisting in the excavation work. At the time of the volcanic eruption there were 15 farmhouses in this part of Þjórsárdalur. It is well worth taking the 30-minute walk from Stöng to see the **Gjáin** gorge and the splendid **Gjár-foss** waterfall.

GULLFOSS

The road continues northward via **Flúðir** (110km/68 miles) to ★★**Gullfoss waterfall** (140km/87 miles). Here the Hvítá river, whose waters originate on the Langjökull glacier, drops a total of 32m (104ft) in two stages, deep into the **Gullfossgljúfur** gorge.

Below: boiling pools at Geysir
Bottom: spouting Strokkur

On sunny afternoons it becomes clear why it is sometimes called the 'Golden Waterfall'. A monument recalls the courageous Sigríður Tómasdóttir (1871–1957), the daughter of a farmer from neighbouring Brattholt. She prevented the authorities from building a hydro-electric power station here, even though a British company had already signed the initial contract.

THE GREAT GEYSER

The geothermal region in the **Haukadalur** (146km/90 miles) is often described by its best-known spouting spring, the ★★**Stóri-Geysir** (Great Geyser, *see box*). Its neighbour, ★★**Strokkur**, reaches only about a third of the Great Geyser's height, but can be relied upon to eject a jet of boiling hot water every few minutes.

Some of the other spouts around the site can discharge columns of very hot water, so it is important to watch where you walk and to read the notice boards.

In **Laugarvatn** (Hot Spring Lake; 180km/112 miles) a popular sauna draws its energy from the hot springs by the lake of the same name. There are several boarding schools in the village that become hotels in summer.

The First Parliament

Þingvallavatn is the second-largest lake in Iceland (exceeded in size only recently by the Þórisvatn reservoir; *see page 94*). ★★ **Þingvellir** (205km/127 miles) on its western shores, lies at the heart of a 50-sq. km (19-sq. mile) national park, opened in 1928. In 930 all the free men on the island met here for the first sitting of the Alþing, the same Icelandic parliament that assembles in Reykjavík today. The site, of great importance to Icelanders, has no surviving buildings to admire, just some foundations to remind visitors of the *búðir* (booths), the shelters and meeting places where representatives conducted business.

> **The Speaker**
> In the early days of the Icelandic Parliament, the laws passed were not written down, but were recited by the Speaker at every session – a narrative that could last several days. It was considered a great honour to be chosen for this important task.

Öxarárfoss waterfall at Þingvellir

A rock served as the official podium during parliamentary sessions. Every year in front of the assembly the parliament's speaker read out the law of the land *(see box)*, a wall of rock providing an acoustic aid. When the assembly was in session – usually once a year for 14 days – the legislators lived in tents and small huts. The **Öxará** river was diverted to improve the water supply. It now pours over into the ★ **Almannagjá** gorge *(see pages 9 and 39)* and flows right past the old parliament site.

The Church

The Parliament did not have a permanent assembly room until the 17th century. To make up for the absence of any historical buildings on the site, a **church** was constructed in 1859 and then, in two stages during the 20th century (1930 and 1974), the five-gabled **Þingvallabær** was added. This is used by the national park rangers and church pastors. It is also available as a summer residence for Iceland's prime minister.

The History of the Nation

Þingvellir links together all the important dates in Icelandic history. With the introduction of Christianity in the year 1000, the old gods were given a good send-off here. In 1262 Icelanders gathered at the site and declared their loyalty to the Norwegian crown.

Until the end of the 18th century, Þingvellir was the venue for the Lögrétta legislative committee, the last bulwark of the parliamentary system under an autocratic monarchy. Even though the Alþing and the Lögrétta had moved to Reykjavík many years before, in 1874 the Icelanders adopted a new constitution here, formally removing power from the Danish crown. At the same time the nation celebrated its first 1,000 years. The new republic was proclaimed here in 1944 and in 1994 Iceland's 50th anniversary as an independent nation was marked by great celebrations.

EVERYMAN'S GORGE

From the north shore of Þingvallavatn a field of lava, restricted by two rifts, stretches deep inland: ★ **Almannagjá**, beside the old assembly in the west, and the less dramatic **Hrafnagjá** in the east. The Almannagjá, or Everyman's Gorge, is 7km (4 miles) long and in some places it was wide enough to accommodate all the free men in the first Icelandic republic.

At **Mosfellsbær** (240km/149 miles) you join the northbound Ring Road. It is now 10km (7 miles) back to **Reykjavík**.

Star Attraction
● **The Parliament**

Below: Icelandic sheep
Bottom: Þingvellir

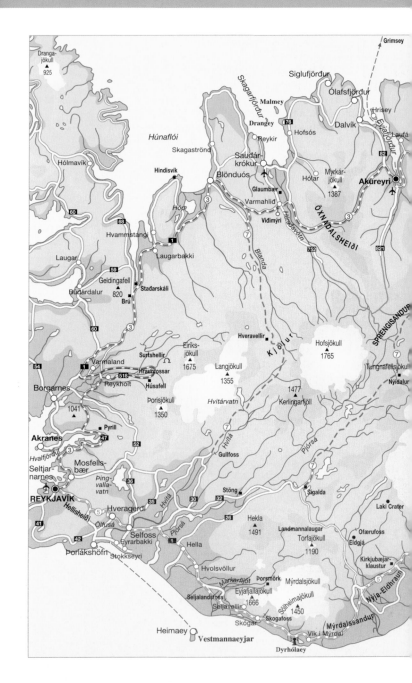

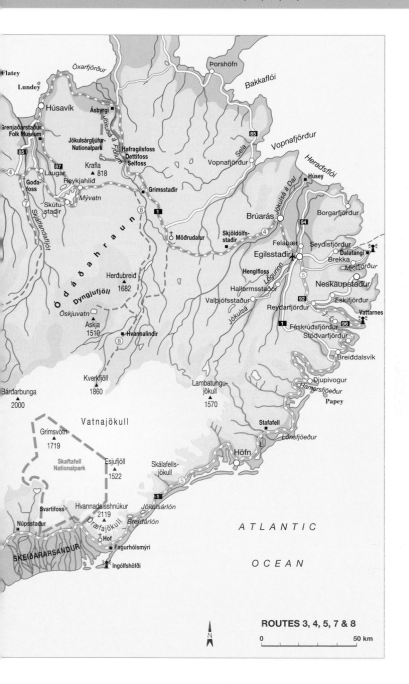

ROUTES 3, 4, 5, 7 & 8

0   50 km

Map on pages 40–1

3: Reyjkavík to Akureyri

Reykjavík – Húsafell – Akureyri (500km/310 miles)

Apart from just one or two detours, this route follows the northern half of the Ring Road on its way to Akureyri, the largest town in Iceland outside the greater Reykjavík area, and passes close to deeply carved fjords and broad bays. Beyond Akureyri, an important staging post, lie the famous Goðafoss waterfall and Mývatn Lake, a paradise for birdwatchers and one of the most volcanically active areas on earth. The further you penetrate into the northeast, the lonelier, the more inhospitable and the more fascinating the landscape becomes.

You should set aside at least three days for this route but, if possible, allow longer. A bus service operates from Reykjavík to Akureyri and on to Egilsstaðir, following the Ring Road, as does this route.

Saga escape
Þyrill Mountain is the setting for an exciting episode in one of the Settlement-era sagas. The daughter of one of the chieftains saves herself and her sons from pirates after a daring escape up the mountain.

Beacon on the cliffs

HOT WATER POINT

Leave **Reykjavík** through the suburb of **Mosfellsbær**. Some of Reykjavík's hot water comes from the geothermal springs here. The long **Hvalfjörður** or 'Whale Fjord' can be reached from the foot of the 909-m (2,982-ft) high Mount Esja, where during the winter there is good skiing on the eastern slopes. The Ring Road follows the tunnel, completed in 1998, under the fjord (toll charge ISK 1,000), but Route 3 follows Highway 47 around the fjord. Overlooking the northern shores is **Þyrill** mountain. A little further along beside the fjord is Iceland's only remaining **whaling station**, but it is currently not in service.

REYKHOLT

Near the Ferstikla roadside service area (81km/50 miles), Route 3 leaves the Ring Road and follows Highways 50 and 518 to **Reykholt** (124km/77 miles). This was the home of Snorri Sturluson

Star Attraction ●
Hraunfossar

(1206–41), the outstanding man of letters of medieval Scandinavia and powerful chieftain who was assassinated at the behest of the king of Norway. His monument, created by Gustav Vigeland in 1947, stands in front of the old school building. Excavations in Reykolt have uncovered a number of medieval foundations, including Snorri's bathing pool.

It is definitely worth stopping to see ★★ **Hraunfossar** (Lava Waterfall; 143km/88 miles), situated 6km (4 miles) west of Húsafell. A small river flows underground above impermeable strata up to the bank of a larger river. Water bubbles out from the lava across a wide expanse between moss, grass and shrubs.

HUSAFELL

★ **Húsafell** (148km/91 miles) is a popular holiday destination for Icelanders and many summer homes nestle in the woods. The settlement is a good starting point for excursions into the Arnarvatnsheiði walking area, and offers swimming pools, hot pools and steam baths. In summer snow-mobiles leave a mountain cabin 18km (11 miles) southeast of Húsafell for the ice-cap of the 1,400-m (4,600-ft) high Langjökull. Daily excursions are also organised from Reykjavík. For information contact Destination Iceland *(see page 110)*.

Below and bottom: tumbling falls of Hraunfossar

Map on pages 40–1

Wayside halt

For over a hundred years travellers have interrupted their journey in Staðarskáli, (274km/170 miles), which lies about halfway between Reykjavík and Akureyri, the two most important population centres in Iceland. A primitive coaching station during the 19th century, the settlement has become a modern staging post, which has even been the subject for poetry and songs. Staðarskáli is now almost a synonym for a roadside service area.

VARMALAND

Highway 518 swings round in a broad curve close to the uninhabited uplands and then heads west, affording some incredible views over the dome-shaped **Eiríksjökull** ice-cap. Near the Fljótstunga farmstead (154km/95 miles), a track forks off to the Surtshellir and Stefánshellir lava caves (guided tours from Húsafell). Shortly before the Ring Road (203km/125 miles), a side road leads to the educational and agricultural centre at **Varmaland**. As well as a swimming pool, thermal bath and campsite, there are some small shops where locally grown produce is sold.

GRABROK

It is worth making the arduous climb through the cinders to the **Grábrók** crater (216km/134 miles) for the view alone. The road climbs slowly but steadily to Holtavörðuheiði at an altitude of over 400m (1,300ft). In severe winters the Ring Road in this highland valley can be blocked off by snow for days. At these times northern and southern Iceland are linked only by air.

The town of **Reykir** (288km/178 miles) lies north of the Ring Road beside Hrútafjörður, an arm of Húnaflói bay and formerly a centre for Icelandic shark fishing, the main theme of Reykir's local history museum.

Hvítserkur

HVAMMSTANGI

A detour to **Hvammstangi** (302km/187 miles) starts just past **Laugarbakki**. The 75-km (45-mile) long road hugs the coast of the Vatnsnes peninsula. The highlights along this stretch are **Hamarsrétt** seaside sheep-fold, where in autumn local farmers meet to sort out ownership of the sheep and horses; **Hindisvík** seal bay almost at the northern tip of the peninsula; and, on its eastern shores, **Hvítserkur**, a rock shrouded in legend resembling a petrified dragon *(see picture, left)*. The coast road meets up with the Ring Road near **Bogarvirki**, the only medieval fortress on Iceland. This is no powerful fortification, but some unspectacular walls reinforce this natural hideout on the crest of a hill.

HÓP

Hóp is a tidal lake, which increases in size by about a third at high tide. The small stone church of Þingeyrar on the eastern shore marks the spot where one of Iceland's most important spiritual centres, a Benedictine monastery, stood during the Middle Ages. In the Skagafjörður hinterland, a lane leads to the turf-covered church of **Víðimýri**, which dates from 1834. The nearby settlement of **Varmahlíð** (405km/251 miles) near hot springs can provide travellers with fuel, roadside services, a supermarket with tourist information in summer, a hotel, a post office and, of course, a swimming pool.

FOLK MUSEUM

While the Ring Road crosses the barren 535-m (1,755-ft) high **Öxnadalsheiði**, before descending to the slender **Hraundrangar** rocky spire and **Eyjafjörður** within easy reach of **Akureyri**, Varmahlíð marks the starting point for a number of diversions and detours of various lengths.

The ★★ **Glaumbær Folk Museum** (open summer daily 9am–6pm) lies about 7km (4 miles) north of Varmahlíð on Highway 75. The former vicarage is a typical example of the building style

Bottom and below: church at Þingeyrar

Map on pages 40–1

adopted in rural areas before the 20th century. The central section consists of adjoining turf-covered houses, each with only one room. Despite the size of the farm, living space was limited, as is clear from the *baðstofa*, the largest room in Glaumbær. Not only did up to 22 people sleep on the 11 beds, many also had to work sitting on them.

Sauðárkrókur was founded in the late 19th century. This town, with a population of about 2,600, is the second most important settlement in northern Iceland after Akureyri. A major attraction is the boat excursions to the striking, rocky island of ★ **Drangey**, which during the summer is a favourite haunt of puffins.

Horse play

The Skagafjörður region is famous throughout Iceland for horse breeding. In the latter part of September, the animals are all brought down from the upland summer pastures for winter. If you are in the area at this time of year, be sure not to miss this colourful event.

Hofsós museum

HÓLAR

Between the years 1106 and 1810 **Hólar** was, after Skálholt, Iceland's second diocese. It was from here that the forces of Catholicism in Scandinavia made their last stand against the Reformation. Bishop Jón Arason stood up to the new movement sweeping Europe and became a folk hero until he and two of his two sons paid with their lives for their obstinacy *(see page 35)*. Iceland's only baroque sandstone church, consecrated in 1763, is a reminder of more illustrious times. An agricultural college, which doubles in the summer as a tourist information office, a basic hostel and a cafeteria, dominates the town.

There is an impressive coastal landscape to appreciate between **Hofsós** – with its restored trading post dating from the Danish Trade Monopoly (1777), now a local history museum, and the Icelandic Emigration Museum (Vesturfarasafnið á Hofsósi) – and the former herring capital of **Siglufjörður**. The local museum is unique – it is the only one in the world that focuses exclusively on the herring. Every year in the second half of July a festival recalls the fish that once brought riches to the town.

A short pass (open from late April) cuts through from Siglufjörður to the western shores of the pretty Eyjafjörður inlet, the fishing villages of **Ólafsfjörður** and **Dalvík** and finally Akureyri.

4: Akureyri and Mývatn

**Akureyri – Goðafoss – Mývatn – Egilsstaðir
(275km/170 miles)**

The small town of ★★**Akureyri** (500km/310
miles from Reykjavík), which likes to describe
itself as the capital of northern Iceland, is home
to just under 17,000 inhabitants. It is the largest
town in the country outside the metropolitan area
of Reykjavík and the fourth largest in Iceland (the
other three are in greater Reykjavík). Its role as
the focus for a large part of the island is evident
from its numerous cultural and educational insti-
tutions. Akureyri has Iceland's second university,
a theatre, a number of museums, good sports facilities, including skiing, a busy airport and enough
hotels and restaurants to cope with the summer
influx of tourists. Despite being only 100km (60
miles) from the Arctic Circle, the town enjoys
some of the warmest weather in the country, with
summer often bringing temperatures of 20°C
(68°F) and clear blue skies.

One of the first settlers in the 10th century was
Helgi Magri or Helgi the Lean. A memorial to him
on the northern edge of the town centre makes
an excellent viewpoint. The town first came to
prominence in 1602 when it was an outpost for the
Danish Trade Monopoly. In 1862 the town with

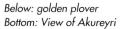

Star Attraction
● **Akureyri**

Below: golden plover
Bottom: View of Akureyri

its 256 inhabitants was granted its municipal charter. After World War II Akureyri underwent a period of growth and a lot of new buildings sprang up around the small town centre. The port, a popular stopping-off point for North Atlantic cruises, is the hub of economic activity. The processing of fish and agricultural products provide employment, as do a chocolate factory and a brewery.

MUSEUMS AND GARDENS

Starting from the tourist information office near the **bus station ❶**, make for the theatre, then continue as far as Aðalstræti. Next to one another there are the **Akureyri Folk Museum ❷** (Minjasafnið; June–mid-September, daily 11am–5pm; mid-September–May, Saturday 2–4pm; admission charge) with an exhaustive collection of local memorabilia, and the **Nonnahús Memorial Museum ❸** (June–August, daily 10am–5pm; winter by arrangment, tel: 462 3555; admission charge). It was here where Reverend Jón 'Nonni' Sveinsson spent five years of his childhood. Nonni wrote a series of books for children about a boy growing up in the north of Iceland based on his own experiences, which were translated into about 40 languages.

When returning to the town centre, call in at the **★★ Botanical Gardens ❹** (Lystigarðurinn), probably the most northerly gardens in the world and Iceland's most attractive garden. Nearly all the country's plants as well as many species from other countries are grown here (June–September, Monday–Friday 8am–10pm, Saturday and Sunday 9am–10pm).

After Einar Jónsson's sculpture *The Outlaw*, a figure looking out towards the fjord with his child on his arm and his (dead) wife over his shoulders, you will come to the **Lutheran church ❺** (daily 10am–noon, 2–4pm), consecrated in 1940. The centre window in the chancel originally graced

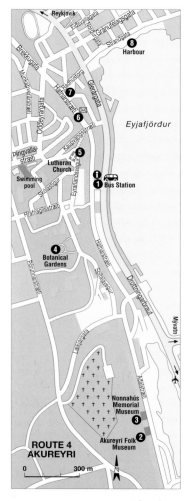

ROUTE 4
AKUREYRI

0   300 m

Coventry Cathedral in the UK. A flight of steps leads from the church's main entrance down to the town centre, where it joins Kaupvangsstræti, known locally as **Listagil** ('Arts Gorge'). At the beginning of the 1990s, some older industrial properties were converted into an interesting collection of studios and meeting rooms, plus the Akureyri Art Gallery (Tuesday–Thursday and Sunday 2–6pm, Friday–Saturday 2–10pm).

Star Attraction
● **Botanical Gardens**

Below: Akureyri church
Bottom: hip city DJ

SHOPPING AND SWIMMING

Instead of touring Akureyri's old buildings and modern churches, you may prefer to pay a visit to the town's swimming pool, which is well supplied with hot pots, plus a large water slide. It is situated at Þingvallastræti 21 above the church.

The northern section of **Hafnarstræti ❻**, now a pedestrian zone, is the town's main shopping street and this leads on to **Rádhústorg ❼** or Town Hall Square. On weekend evenings the young people of Akureyri pay homage to America's cultural influence by ostentatiously cruising round here in their cars. It is only a few metres from here to the **harbour ❽** and Strandgata, where the cruise ships moor during the summer.

Brekkugata, a northward extension of Hafnarstræti, runs north past the sports ground and on to the Helgi Magri memorial *(see page 47)*, which

Map
pages
40–1

is worth a visit for the view alone.

Just south of Akureyri, bridges and causeways carry the main road to the east over the end of Eyjafjörður. The Ring Road then runs along its eastern shores. Initially there are some great views of Akureyri and then of the fjord as the road heads north. Before you turn to the east through a pass down into the Fnjóská valley, take a detour of 12km (7 miles) to the **Laufás** local history museum, which occupies an old vicarage. The turf-covered building was constructed between 1840 and 1866. Some 13 living rooms and communal areas, as well as the timber church, which dates from 1865, are open to the public (mid-May–mid-September, daily 10am–6pm).

★ **Goðafoss** or Waterfall of the Gods (549km/341 miles) does not fall a great distance but it is an amazing sight as rocks split up the surging water flow of the Skjálfandafljót river into several sections. The name derives from the early Christian era when a local chieftain threw carvings of the Norse gods into the river.

Below: Laufás history museum
Bottom: Goðafoss

GRIMSEY

Unlike many of the offshore islands, **Grímsey**, about 40km (25 miles) from the mainland to the north of Akureyri, is inhabited. About 100 people, including youngsters, earn a living from the still well-stocked fishing grounds. Before a telephone line was laid in 1931, a supply boat called in twice a year with provisions. Now there is a runway and a Twin Otter can fly from Akureyri in 20 minutes.

Grímsey is the only part of Iceland on the Arctic Circle (66° 30' N). Birding enthusiasts come to see the plentiful puffins and the rarer little auk. **Básar** (tel: 467 3103) can offer beds, space for sleeping bags and simple meals.

LAUGAR

Laugar (558km/346 miles) is not an attraction in itself, but it does make a good alternative base for exploring the Mývatn region about 30km (19 miles) away.

LAKE MÝVATN

Soon after Laugar the road reaches a small lake (573km/ 356 miles), set amid a barren landscape. Tour guides relate the story of some Americans who returned a hire car to Akureyri, complaining about how boring Mývatn was, but the mileometer revealed that the vehicle had barely come as far as this lake, the Másvatn. It is only beyond the next range of hills that ★★★ **Lake Mývatn** comes into view. Initially, you will encounter its outflow, the Laxá – this river is the preferred breeding-ground for the harlequin duck and the Barrow's goldeneye duck, two species that have arrived here from America. This is the only European breeding ground for the latter species. The whole area is extremely active volcanically.

Star Attraction
● Lake Mývatn

Expensive fish
The Laxá river is famous for its salmon and trout, and notorious for the extortionate cost of fishing permits.

ROUTE 4
MÝVATN

0   2 km

Map
on page
51

Midge lake

Mývatn means 'the midge lake'. The evidence for this is clearly visible on windless days in June and August – less so in July – when swarms of these tiny flies swirl above the water close to the shore. They are, of course, a vital source of food for the lake's bird life. One consolation is that very few of the flies are biters, one of which is the female blackfly, which only lives by the banks of the Laxá. Nevertheless, the non-biting majority certainly make their presence felt. They exist in such numbers that they penetrate into the nose, the eyes, even the ears.

A GREEN OASIS

The Ring Road soon reaches **Skútustaðir** (587km/364 miles) and the **★★ Skútustaðagígar** pseudo-crater at the edge of the lake. These were formed when water trapped beneath flowing lava, boiled and burst up through the surface, creating what looks like volcanic cones. Some were formed so recently that their sides are still charred.

One of the most attractive spots by Mývatn is **Höfði** woodland park (595km/370 miles), on a spit jutting out into the lake. Compared to the rest of Iceland with its bleak landscape, this green corner is like a primeval forest. The view from Höfði extends out over the lake taking in the bizarre lava pillars, the distinctive symbols for Lake Mývatn.

More unusual shapes can be seen at **Dimmuborgir** (Black Castles; 595km/370 miles and then another 2km/1¼ miles to the car park), a vast, 2,000-year-old field of contorted volcanic pillars, some extending as high as 20 metres (65 ft). There is a viewing platform over the expanse and visitors can wander about among the haunting arches, caves and natural tunnels. Dimmuborgir was formed when the Þrengslaborgir series of craters further east erupted. An obstacle caused the molten lava to form into a lake, which then cooled unevenly. Eventually the blockage gave way and the lava that was still in liquid form flowed away leaving behind this strange landscape.

Lake Mývatn

HVERFELL

The prominent and evenly formed tephra gravel ring, **Hverfell** (595km/370 miles), has nothing to do with molten lava. Standing a good 180m (590ft) above the surrounding terrain, it can easily be reached on foot (about 2km/1¼ miles) by someone in good shape – a worthwhile, if dusty, experience. It is a much longer walk to the **Lúdent**, Hverfell's counterpart. Both of these are the result of short but very violent eruptions. **Lúdentsborgir** and **Þrengslaborgir**, a series of craters to the south, are also examples of this type of volcano.

You have to pass this way to get to one of the most mysterious sites in the region, the 60-m (196-ft) deep basalt-pillared gorge of ★ **Seljahjallagil**. Although it is in ecological terms a very sensitive area, the gorge is open to tourism. It can be reached as part of a day hike, but visitors are requested to be very careful. It is also possible to explore the gorge under expert guidance as part of a tour starting in Reykjahlíð.

Reykjahlíð (600km/372 miles) is the main tourist centre for Lake Mývatn. The huge plates of lava which surround the village, and the village church in particular, make a fascinating sight. The previous church was miraculously spared during the Great Mývatn Fire (1724–29). Because it stood on a low and barely perceptible rise, the flow parted and missed the church by only a few metres. Other examples of volcanic phenomena are the hot-spring caves at **Stóragjá**, situated beside the Ring Road, and **Grjótagjá**, beside a track a few kilometres to the southwest. Dramatic changes in water temperature have occurred in past years as a result of activity way below the earth's surface.

ENVIRONMENTAL CONCERNS

The next section of this route as far as Egilsstaðir is often closed in winter. There's a good chance of snow from mid-September until well into May. On the outskirts of Reykjahlíð is a factory that uses geothermal energy to process the diatoms in Lake Mývatn's sediment into diatomite, a raw material used in industrial filters, insulating mat-

Star Attraction
● Skútustaðagígar

Below: Reykjahlíð church
Bottom: grazing on volcanic ground near Lake Mývatn

Map on pages 40–1

erials and cosmetics. The removal of the minuscule diatoms is a controversial issue; dredging operations definitely have an effect on lake's ecosystem, but the long-term impact is not clear.

Below: Námaskarð thermal area
Bottom: Krafla Power Station

STICKY MUD

At the foot of ★ **Námaskarð** (605km/375 miles) lies **Hverarönd**, one of Iceland's best-known geothermal fields, with sulphur deposits and a series of mud pots and steam vents. During the colonial era, the Danish kings extracted sulphur for gunpowder here. It is a sensible idea to wrap plastic bags around your shoes as the mud near the springs is sticky and difficult to scrape off.

A side road (7km/4 miles) off the solfatara field opposite goes to **Krafla** and its explosion crater known as Víti (Hell). A power station there converts energy from the earth's core into electricity, and its construction in 1973 may have triggered the many eruptions that have occurred since. The whole lifeless, primeval area gives as good a glimpse of the fresly formed earth as you ever are likely to get, but be aware of the risks.

Just under 30km (19 miles) north of Grímsstaðir (campsite; 639km/397 miles) is **Dettifoss** *(see page 57)*, the biggest waterfall in Europe and definitely worth the detour along the minor Highway 864.

There is a longer, alternative route for the stretch between Reykjahlíð and Grímsstaðir (an additional 145km/90 miles and at least one extra day). Leave the Mývatn region in a northerly direction towards Húsavík. Just off the main road is the **Grenjaðarstaður Folk Museum** in a turf-covered farmhouse that dates from the mid-19th century.

HÚSAVÍK

Húsavík (pop. 2,500) is an important town in this part of northern Iceland and is Iceland's whale-watching capital. In summer the waters off Húsavík swarm with whales and ★★ **whale-watching excursions** are almost guaranteed success. Occasionally, even blue whales are sighted; and in August the impressive humpback whales appear in these waters, too. An informative **Whale Centre** (tel: 464 2520, www.icewhale.is; May and September, daily 10am–6pm; June–August, daily 9am–7pm) has been set up in Húsavík harbour and doubles as a tourist information centre. Two companies take whale enthusiasts out to sea – sometimes as many as nine times a day. Norður Sigling (tel: 464 2350, www.nordursigling.is; 3 hours, about ISK3,800) has two beautifully restored oak cutters which are ideal for such excursions, while the other company, Gentle Giants (tel: 464 1500, www.gentlegiants.is; 3 hours, ISK3,700) uses a former whale-hunting boat for the whale excursions.

Húsavík, meaning 'House Bay', likes to describe itself as the first Norse settlement on Iceland. According to old manuscripts, Garðar Svavarsson spent a winter here 14 years before the first permanent settlers arrived.

POLAR BEARS AND PHALLI

Dominating the town above the harbour is the two-storey, cross-shaped timber church, built in 1907. **Safnahúsið**, the local museum (Stórigarður), has a natural history collection that includes a stuffed polar bear. It is said that drift ice brought the animal to the Icelandic coast from eastern Greenland during a severe winter.

Star Attraction
● **Whalewatching**

Swimming sense
It you are unsure whether it is safe to bathe in one of the caves, seek advice locally. But remember that if you do bathe in one of these naturally heated pools, you will be swimming in warm, unchlorinated water after hundreds of other bathers. A far more hygienic option is to pay a visit to the modern thermal baths with some relaxing hot pots at the eastern end of Reykjahlið.

Boats, Húsavík

Map
on pages
40–1

While in Húsavík, visit the motley collection of penises that is the **Icelandic Phallological Museum** (late May–early September daily noon–6pm) at Heðinbraut 3a. Specimens range from whales to rams; a human penis has (thankfully) so far evaded the collector.

On boat excursions from Húsavík and during the onward journey along Highway 85 around the Tjörnes peninsula, you will see the island of **Lundey** – the name means Puffin Island and many of these birds nest here. Below you on the east side of the peninsula lies the broad **Öxarfjörður** inlet with the most striking sandur (spit formations) in northern Iceland. Jökulsá á Fjöllum, a huge glacial river originating on the northern edge of Vatna-jökull, formed this part of Iceland over many thousands of years. Back in the mists of time, ★★ **Ásbyrgi** was a waterfall, but then a volcanic eruption or an earthquake changed the course of the river and a horseshoe-shaped gorge, opening out to the sea and closed off from the interior by rock faces up to 100m (330ft) high, was left behind.

Below: Ásbyrgi gorge
Bottom: Dettifoss

ICELAND'S GRAND CANYON

★★ **Jökulsárgljúfur National Park**, of which Ásbyrgi is a part, is often described as Iceland's Grand Canyon. The park lines a most impressive river course some 25km (16 miles) long, up

to 120m (400ft) deep and 500m (1,650ft) wide. At many points its walls are decorated with basalt columns or arches, interspersed with huge basalt sculptures, all shaped over thousands of years by the Jökulsá á Fjöllum river.

There is a series of spectacular waterfalls along the length of the canyon. From a viewpoint near Highway 864 it is possible to get a bird's eye view of **Hafragilsfoss**. A little further on a road leads up to ★★ **Dettifoss**, Europe's most prolific waterfall. The water of the Jökulsá, coloured grey by tons of sediment, cascades down 44m (150ft) at a spellbinding rate of 500 cubic metres per second. A short walk upriver is **Selfoss** waterfall, not quite so spectacular, but still photogenic. This alternative route rejoins the Ring Road near Grímsstaðir.

SÆNAUTASEL FARMHOUSE

As the road heads eastward, the landscape becomes lonelier and increasingly barren. The farm at **Möðrudalur** (674km/418 miles) is the highest (470m/1,541ft) and one of the most remote in the country. When the tiny church appears out of the wilderness, it is a welcoming sight.

The next 45km (28 miles) passes through a desert of gravel and ash with almost no vegetation, a landscape very similar to the central highlands. A gem in this desolate part of the country is the turf-covered ★★ **Sænautasel** farmhouse (698km/433 miles), which was re-opened in 1994 after 50 years of gradual decay. Built in 1843, it has been lovingly restored and is now used as a café in summer. Walking towards it, you cross a stream via a bridge that is a small-scale but accurate reconstruction of an 18th-century bridge that crossed the Jökulsá á Brú river. Near the school at **Brúarás**, used in the summer as inexpensive accommodation, plus cafeteria, the grey water squeezes through a deep and narrow canyon.

At this point Iceland's highest bridge crosses the river. This one was built in 1994 to replace its dilapidated 1930s predecessor. According to local legend, there was a natural bridge here that survived until the 16th century, when it collapsed. At

Star Attractions
● **Ásbyrgi**
● **Dettifoss**

> **Busy river**
> The Jökulsá á Brú glacial river, which the road follows for many kilometres, sweeps up to 120 tonnes of sand and gravel per hour from a large area at the northeastern corner of Vatnajökull out to sea, thus creating one of Iceland's busiest conveyor belts.

Remote church near Möðrudalur

Map
on pages
40–1

River or lake?
Is the Lögurinn a river or a lake? Its waters move slowly but steadily towards the sea, the milky grey colour revealing that it is meltwater from the northern edge of the Vatnajökull ice-cap. Many visitors scan the water in vain for the legendary giant worm, Lagarfljótsormur – according to descriptions, a close relative of Nessie, Scotland's Loch Ness monster.

Reindeer grazing on Mount Snæfell

the end of that century, Hanseatic merchants paid for Iceland's first human-built bridge.

THE EASTERN CAPITAL

At **Fellabær** (770km/478 miles) the **Lagarfljót**, as the outflow of Lögurinn is called, is crossed by a 300-m (1,000-ft) long wooden bridge. On the other side of the bank lies **Egilsstaðir** (775km/481 miles), the modern but faceless 'capital' of eastern Iceland and the final destination for this route. Just over 2,800 people now live in what is the most important town in this region.

Certainly more attractive than the town itself is the surrounding area, above all the pencil-shaped lake of **Lögurinn**, which is just under 40km (25 miles) long, up to 2km (1¼ miles) wide and in places 112m (370ft) deep. Near **Hallormsstaður** you can take a forest walk in Iceland's largest woodland area. A reafforestation program here might be extended to other parts of Iceland to return them to their pre-Viking state of being 'covered by woods from mountain to shore'. At the southern end of the lake stands the church at **Valþjófsstaður** that has a copy of a medieval wooden door. The original, one of the most precious pieces of wood-carving in the country, is kept in the National Museum in Reykjavík.

GUNNAR GUNNARSSON

To the north at **Skriðuklaustur**, the former home of the Icelandic writer Gunnar Gunnarsson (1889–1975) can be seen on the site of an old monastery. Gunnarsson's reputation is still disputed in Iceland, as he had sympathies with Nazi Germany, where he enjoyed his greatest literary success – a fate he shared with the Norwegian Nobel prize-winner, Knut Hamsun. It is said that the house, built in 1939, was designed by Hitler's favourite architect, Höger.

A track that is only suitable for 4-wheel-drive vehicles branches off to the permanently snow-covered **Snæfell** and to the northern edge of **Vatnajökull**, one of the toughest regions for hikers anywhere in Iceland. A little further on from the bridge over the Hengifossá marks the start of a good 2-hour walk along the river to the basalt-columned ★ **Litlanesfoss** and ★ **Hengifoss** water-falls. Return to Egilsstaðir via Fellabær.

Star Attraction
● Seyðisfjörður

FERRY PORT

The harbour for the ferry that links Iceland with the rest of Europe is at ★★ **Seyðisfjörður**, one of Iceland's few truly attractive coastal towns. Its charming houses around the jetty date from the boom years of the 19th century when Norwegian fish merchants had bases here. Seyðisfjörður obtained its municipal charter in 1895. Since then its population has dwindled to around 800.

As the ferry to the European mainland sails on Thursday (late May–early September; rest of the year departure is on Wednesday; www.smyril-line.com), accommodation in the area is full to capacity prior to its departure. An arts and crafts market and classical and jazz concerts are held mid-week to coincide with the influx of visitors. If you are not intending to catch the ferry, avoid the Egilsstaðir/Seyðisfjörður area on Wednesday and Thursday. Whatever your plans, it is essential to book mid-week accommodation in advance. The Skaftfell arts centre (Austurvegur 42) is a widely-celebrated non-profit art gallery (open all summer, check in advance during winter; www.skaftfell.is).

Below: hiking near Hengifoss
Bottom: near Seyðisfjörður

Map on pages 40–1

5: Iceland's East and South

Egilsstaðir – Reyðarfjörður – Höfn – Vatnajökull – Kirkjubæjarklaustur – Vík – Reykjavík (750km/466 miles)

This route begins with a journey along the East fjords. Although the attractions of this landscape are obvious, they are still to be discovered by many visitors to Iceland. The road runs through an impressive fjord landscape beneath several striking mountain peaks. To the south of Djúpivogur it runs beside a series of lagoons. Narrow spits of gravel and sand deposited by the glacial rivers push out between the bays and the open sea.

Below: Vatnajökull
Bottom: rhyolitic hills typical of Landmannalaugur

HÖFN

Höfn marks the start of the south coast. For the next 150km (93 miles) this route follows closely one of the most spectacular landscapes on earth: the Vatnajökull ice-cap with its many valley glaciers, drifting icebergs on the Jökulsárlón glacial lake and the dramatic Skaftafell National Park. The route also offers plenty of opportunities for detours, such as a tour of the colourful rhyolite mountains of Landmannalaugur. Another possibility is a foray to the Þorsmörk

valley, framed by beautiful glaciers and fast-flowing glacial rivers.

A bus service links Egilsstaðir, Höfn and Reykjavík. Public transport also covers all the detours described in this route. While the Ring Road follows the shorter route over the 470m (1,541ft) high Breiðdalsheiði to the Breið-dalur valley, Route 5 leaves Egilsstaðir *(see page 58)* to the southeast along good, mainly asphalt roads by the fjords. When the fjord road rejoins the Ring Road in Breiðdalsvík, you will have done an extra 145km (90 miles).

CHALLENGING HEIGHTS

Do not expect to see anything spectacular by the **Mjóifjörður inlet**, but nature lovers will enjoy it. The 600-m (1,975-ft) high, bare and inhospitable Mjóafjarðarheiði is tempting for climbers and there could be snow on the ground at almost any time in the year. The road then snakes its way down to the fjord passing waterfalls.

Only about 30 people still live beside the fjord, most of them in **Brekka**. Situated here are the church, dating from 1892, and a school. In the summer the dormitories become the basic but cosy Sólbrekka accommodation, which has a cafeteria (tel: 476 0007).

DALATANGI

At the beginning of the 20th century, Mjóifjörður was one of the busiest settlements in eastern Iceland. Once 700 people lived here, staffing one of the country's first cold-storage warehouses. Some of the first telephones were installed here and for many years there was a small, private electricity generating station.

A track running tantalisingly close to the steep slopes that overlook the fjord goes as far as **Dalatangi**. At one time there were seven farmhouses here, now only one of them is inhabited. The lighthouse keeper's residence belongs to the nation. Beside the new lighthouse stands the ruin of Iceland's first coastal beacon.

> **Troll tales**
> A female troll, said to have once lived in the Prestagil ravine near Brekka, would often lay in wait for priests, who made a tasty snack. More appetising, however, are the blueberries that grow at lower altitudes and can be picked in late August.

Waterfall at the Mjóifjörður inlet

Map on pages 40–1

VATTARNES

The main route follows the coast. If you follow the suggested route you will reach the easternmost point of your round trip at **Vattarnes** lighthouse (64km/40 miles). Birding enthusiasts should continue for a few more kilometres and ask at the Vattnes farmhouse (tel: 475 1397) if there are likely to be any boat trips to the **Skrúður** bird rock, which lies offshore.

Fáskrúðsfjörður (81km/50 miles) has, like many fjord settlements, to cope with two names. The village is usually referred to by the name of the adjacent fjord, less often by its true place name, Buðir. Between 1880 and 1935 it was the base for a small French fishing colony. The many graves in the old cemetery at Fáskrúðsfjörður remind visitors of those times. Above the southern shores of the fjord towers the 743-m (2,437-ft) rhyolite Sandfell mountain.

The small village of **Stöðvarfjörður** (110km/68 miles) bears the alternative name of Kirkjuból.

Rock garden
Just before leaving the village of Kirkjuból in the direction of Breiðdalsvík, you will pass the unusual stone and mineral collection that Petra Sveinsdóttir has painstakingly assembled in her garden.

Arctic fox

COASTAL DETOUR

After a breathtaking stretch of road which crosses the steep Kambaskriður slopes high up above the coast, the route rejoins the Ring Road in **Breiðdalsvík** (130km/80 miles) and then continues on towards Reykjavík. The road follows a southbound course along the shores of the Breiðdalsvík inlet. At Berunes Youth Hostel (152km/94 miles), the village of Djúpivogur comes into view on the other side of the fjord.

Djúpivogur is less than 5km (3 miles) away, but the ★★ **Berufjörður** inlet sends motorists on a time-consuming detour. The coast road is some 40km (25 miles) long, but the superb mountain panorama of ridges and rugged peaks, in particular the 1,000-m (3,250-ft) high Búlandstindur pyramid above **Djúpivogur** (192km/120 miles), compensate for the extra distance. This village, the last place of any size before Höfn, a good 100km (60 miles) away by road, was a trading post for German merchants at the end of the 16th century.

PAPEY

The Ring Road runs around the edge of the settlement. Take a turning to the left to reach the centre of the village. The decent harbour here makes a good base for fishing and trade and provides a living for the 600 or so inhabitants. It is an important centre as, apart from Heimaey on the Westman Islands, there is only one other mainland harbour, the one at Höfn, between here and Þorlákshöfn, which is a short distance from Reykjavík.

To the southeast of Djúpivogur lies the tiny island of ★ **Papey**, now inhabited only by thousands of sea birds. The name indicates that even before the first Norse settlers had arrived on Iceland, Celtic monks, possibly Irish, known in the Viking language as *papen*, lived here. Relics of the community that once lived here include the smallest and oldest wooden church in the country, believed to date from 1807. For information about accommodation and organised tours to the island, contact Papeyjarferðir on tel: 478 8838.

OBSTRUCTIVE INLETS

The next inlet to the south, **Hamarsfjörður**, is a fjord in name, but this is where the straight coastline typical of the whole of southeast Ice-

Star Attraction
● Berufjörður

Below: hardy Icelander
Bottom: fjord on the
east coast

Map on pages 40–1

Sunset view
If the weather is fine, try to arrange your day so that you can watch the sunset from the Almannaskarð pass – it's an incredible sight.

Looking towards Vatnajökull

land, begins. Where the fjord meets the sea, currents deposit banks of sand and gravel so that spits and lagoons form, making navigation in the inshore waters almost impossible.

Near **Álftafjörður** and particularly the **Lón** lagoon, spit formation is well advanced. These spits are what geologists refer to as sandurs, flat expanses of outwash formed from sediment. Here it is the glacial rivers rising on Vatnajökull and several other smaller glaciers that have caused the build-up.

The **Austurhorn** (245km/152 miles), the northern limit of Lón, is a sugar loaf mountain formed from gabbro, a stone that is quite rare in Iceland. Unlike the surface rock which predominates elsewhere, gabbro is a deep-earth rock, similar to granite.

VIEW FROM THE TOP

The farmhouse at **Stafafell í Lón** (263km/163 miles) is a good base for those wishing to explore the impressive uplands at the eastern edge of Vatnajökull, the **Lónsöræfi** peaks – rugged and, in places, glaciated remnants of a central volcano dating from the tertiary era and an opportunity for some demanding walks.

The **Almannaskarð** pass (282km/175 miles) is the steepest section of the Ring Road. Do stop and admire the magnificent view from the top. On a promontory, which separates the Hornafjörður and Skarpsfjörður lagoons, lies the town of Höfn. Two elongated spits almost close off the area from the sea. Further west lie seemingly endless sandurs, on top of which ice from Vatnajökull sparkles in the sun.

FISHING SETTLEMENT

★ **Höfn í Hornafirði** (294km/182 miles) is a fishing village founded just under 100 years ago. In 1974 when the southern half of the Ring Road was completed and the land route to Reykjavík was no longer via Akureyri, the town enjoyed a boost to its prosperity. Höfn, with its 1,600 inhabitants, is the largest town on the Ring Road between Akureyri and Selfoss, still a distance of more than 900km (560 miles). Most visitors come here to join the summer 'Glacier Tour', which includes snowcatting and a visit to the iceberg-filled lake of Jökusárlón *(see page 66)* in a single, easy trip.

A Seafarers and Fishermen's Memorial, built in 1988, dominates the harbour area – the sea is the main source of employment for the inhabitants of Höfn. This memorial serves as a good viewpoint over the narrow passage between the two spits, which are gradually moving closer together. Fierce currents make the gap that lets boats pass out on to the open sea very dangerous, but it is the only way to reach the fishing grounds.

MOUNTAIN ROADS

It is easy to return to the Ring Road from Höfn (298km/185 miles). At Smyrlabjörg hydro-electric power station (341km/211 miles), a ★ **mountain road**, only passable by conventional vehicles for the first few kilometres, forks off. Leave your car by the power station and travel by four-wheel drive bus (early June to early September, once or twice daily) along the spectacular track up to the Jöklasel mountain base on ★★ **Skálafellsjökull** glacier.

Star Attraction
● **Skálafellsjökull**

Below: speeding on the Skálafellsjökull
Bottom: Vatnajökull

Map
on pages
40-1

*Below and bottom: glacial
lagoon, Jökulsárlón*

VATNAJÖKULL

At an altitude of 840m (2,756ft) stands the
★★★ **Vatnajökull ice-cap**, which is a temperate
glacier: its temperature is at melting point, or
very close to it, at any given depth, except in the
top layers, where frost may remain until far into
the summer. Formed around 2,500 years ago,
it covers one-twelfth of the country. At its edge
is the Jöklasel restaurant, which claims to have
the best view in Iceland – one only bettered by
views from the air. The vista to the south
extends over Höfn, the flat inshore terrain and
the Atlantic Ocean, while only a few metres
away motor sleighs and snowmobiles stand
ready to carry passengers away on an adventure
over the eternal ice.

If you do not wish to go up on to the glacier, then you can still experience the ice, as it
extends down to the Ring Road. During the 19th
century the **Breiðamerkurjökull** ice tongue
(373km/231 miles) used to reach as far as the
sea, but the glacier receded and the deep
★★ **Jökulsárlón** glacial lake and the 1.5-km (1-
mile) long Jökulsá glacial river were formed.
Floating on the lake against the spectacular
backdrop of the huge ice-cap, broken up only
by a few mountain peaks, are countless icebergs,
their blue, white and black colour, dependent on
air and ash content.

Boat trips out onto the world of ice are available throughout the summer months, and there is a cafeteria beside the Jökulsárlón (mid-May–mid-September; tel: 478 2122).

Star Attraction
● **Vatnajökull ice-cap**
● **Jökulsárlón**

GLACIAL LAKE

Not quite so accessible to tourists, but then not quite so spectacular, is the **Breiðárlón** glacial lake (384km/238 miles) at the foot of **Fjallsjökull**. This glacial tongue is creeping down from **Öræfajökull**, the southernmost spur of the Vatnajökull ice-cap. Lying dormant underneath the ice is a volcano, which erupted in 1362 and then again in 1727, devastating the surrounding area on both occasions. **Hvannadalsshnúkur**, a peak that emerges from the Öræfajökull ice-cap, is Iceland's highest mountain (2,119m/6,952ft).

> **Tractor trip**
> Try to make the worthwhile and, for Iceland, relatively inexpensive 2–4 hour excursion by tractor and hay wagon along a spit to the barrier island of Ingólfshöfði (www.hofsnes.com/coast.htm).

At its foot lies the settlement of **Fagurhólsmýri** (405km/251 miles), the centre of the Öræfi region. In the absence of a decent harbour and restricted by the vast glacial rivers to the east and west, the only route to the outside world for the people who lived here was for many centuries over the ice of Vatnajökull.

Ingólfshöfði is where in 874 Ingólfur Arnarson, Iceland's first permanent settler, lived for some time before moving on to Reykjavík. Seals and sea birds are always visible, occasionally whales. Ingólfshöfði is a nature conservation area with the largest puffin colony on the south coast. **Hof** (408km/253 miles) is a small settlement with a pretty turf-covered church.

SKAFTAFELL

It is not far to the entrance to the ★★ **Skaftafell National Park** (428km/265 miles), which occupies a small part of Vatnajökull. Framed by glaciers, this region of woodland and moor is one of Iceland's top sights. There is a campsite and information centre, shop and café, which all get very busy on summer weekends. Allow at least two hours for a walk to the dramatic **Svartifoss** waterfall, which is backed by a wall of basalt columns.

Svartifoss

Map
on pages
40–1

OVERHANGING GLACIER

If you wish to visit Iceland's only overhanging glacier, ★ **Morsárjökull**, set aside at least one day. Ice blocks often break off and crash over a mountain ledge into the valley. Alternatively, you may wish to see where the Skeiðará river emerges from the Skeiðarárjökull. In November 1996, vast quantities of water gushed out from under the glacier, melted by a subglacial volcano, Grímsvötn. Further eruptions in 1998 and 2004 produced extensive clouds of ash and gas but no glacial burst. A detailed brochure showing all the footpaths in the vicinity is available from the information office at the national park's administrative centre.

Stones gathering moss
The Ring Road crosses the expanse of lava to the west of Kirkjubæjarklaustur and is now overgrown with moss. Depending on how much rain has fallen, the block lava appears either as a rich green or a dull grey colour.

GLACIER BURST

Route 5 crosses **Skeiðarársandur**, Iceland's largest sandur, to the west of Skaftafell. In November 1996 about 8km (5 miles) of National Highway 1 were washed away in the *jökulhlaup* or glacier burst from Grímsvötn. Two days later, when the burst came to an end, a million tons of ice had broken away from Skeiðarárjökull glacier, which dominates the view on the north side of the road. Since the glacial burst, the bridges and road have been renewed and restored.

Systrafoss **Lómagnúpur**, the 777-m (2,549-ft) high

cape, marks the western end of Skeiðarársandur. Visible here are the land uplift and also
the sand and gravel, which were deposited at the
same time. In primordial times the sea crashed
against Lómagnúpur's rocks. Situated at its foot
now is the **Núpsstaður** farmstead (462km/287
miles) with its original stable buildings and
charming turf-covered chapel dating from 1659.
From here the coastline runs south for more than
20km (12 miles).

Kirkjubæjarklaustur (495km/307 miles) has
only about 200 inhabitants, but the school and
trading centre serve a wide catchment area. Irish
monks lived here before the arrival of the Norse
settlers. A Benedictine convent survived from
1186 until the Reformation and many of the
names for local geographical features refer to the
nuns. Examples include ★ **Systrastapi** (Sisters'
Rock), ★ **Systrafoss** (Sisters' Waterfall) and **Sys-
travatn** (Sisters' Lake). However, it can't have
been a model institution, since two of the nuns
were burned at the stake: one for sleeping with
the devil, the other for maligning the Pope. Near
Highway 203, which leads to the campsite, is
Kirkjugólf (Church Floor), a smooth surface with
the tops of hexagonal basalt columns fitting
together as perfectly as tiles.

LAKI CRATER

When the Laki crater erupted in 1783 *(see page
18)* in Iceland's worst natural disaster, Kirkjubæjarklaustur would have been destroyed had the
pastor not brought the wall of fire to a standstill
by delivering a passionate sermon. Known as
Nýja-Eldhraun or Fire Lava, the resulting field
of lava covers an area of 550 sq. km (212 sq.
miles) and is the largest recorded lava flow from
one eruption since the Settlement.

The track (501km/311 miles) that leads to the
★★ **Laki crater** is only suitable for four-wheel-
drive vehicles or the special bus (July/August,
daily from Kirkjubæjarklaustur). **Fjarðará
canyon**, however, a spectacular gorge, can be
reached in any vehicle (a further 5km/3 miles).

Star Attraction
● **Laki Crater**

Below: Fjarðará canyon
Bottom: lava formations

Map
on pages
40–1

The Fjarðará river has carved its way through the earth and created a narrow but very deep and craggy canyon – in some places only a few metres wide.

Sandstorms and Volcanoes

The Ring Road now crosses the Kúðafljót glacial river via a new bridge. The kingdom of Vatnajökull now lies behind you; ahead are **Mýrdalsjökull** and the notorious **Mýrdalssandur**. After crossing this sand-and-gravel desert it used to be the custom to leave 'good-luck' cairns made from layers of stone by the roadside. Many modern-day tourists continue this tradition.

Mýrdalssandur's bad name stems from two phenomena. Fierce sandstorms can in extreme cases remove rust, even paint, from a car in much the same way that buildings are cleaned by sandblasting. Beside the road travellers can see how attempts have been made to stabilise the sand with vegetation.

Vigilance and modern scientific methods give some warning about the second danger. Lying dormant beneath the ice of Mýrdalsjökull is the Katla volcano, which has boiled over 16 times since the settlement of Iceland, that is, approximately every 70 years. The last eruption was in 1918, so the next one is now overdue. When the

Mount Katla
Eruptions from subglacial volcanoes can cause more damage than those from open-air volcanoes. Hot lava melts the ice, triggering sudden floods – *hlaups* – with unpredictable results. Mount Katla, the volcano beneath the glacier Mýrdalsjökull, is Iceland's largest caldera, at 80 sq. km (30 sq. miles). When Katla erupts, the *hlaup* can be 200,000 cubic metres (7 million cubic ft) of water a second.

Vík's Reynisdrangar
(Troll Rocks)

volcano becomes active beneath the ice, a devastating wall of water floods Mýrdalssandur. Two mountains tower above this plain. Undoubtedly both were originally islands, which as a result of land uplift and silting have lost contact with the sea.

Nearer to the coast lies **Hjörleifshöfði** (554km/344 miles).

STORM-BATTERED COAST

★★ **Vík í Mýrdal** (566km/352 miles) is a little town of 400 people situated on a dramatic stretch of coastline battered by a relentless wind: here the dark North Atlantic hits the land with surprising violence, its waves crashing dramatically on a long beach of black sand. The town can offer travellers all the amenities they need. Excursions on amphibious vehicles to some dramatic offshore rock formations are available from the Víkurskáli service area (tel: 487 1230).

Although a coastal town, Vík has no harbour because of silting. One of the destinations that can be reached from Vík is Iceland's southern cape, **Dyrhólaey**. There is a striking natural arch, topped by a photogenic lighthouse. Dyrhólaey (Door Hill Island) was originally an underwater volcano, but it grew into an island. Over many thousands of years part of it has merged with the Icelandic mainland. The coast is gradually shifting to the south, as new material from the glacial rivers is deposited on the shores and it is quite possible that in a few hundred years' time hikers will be able to pass through the arch carved by the Atlantic breakers.

A track (581km/361 miles) runs from the Ring Road to the Dyrhólaey plateau; it is well worth making the short journey for the magnificent view it affords of the coast.

By the **Sólheimajökull** glacier (access at 595km/370 miles) lies the centre of glacier tourism on Mýrdalsjökull. Available here are snowmobile excursions, organised by Arcanum (tel: 487 1500; www.snow.is).

Star Attraction
● Vík í Mýrdal

Below: Dyrhólaey
Bottom: Skógar homestead

Map
on pages
40–1

Below: Þórsmörk
Bottom: Seljalandsfoss

SKOGAFOSS

In **Skógar** (601km/373 miles) the 60-m (200-ft) high ★★**Skógafoss** thunders over the cliffs of the old coastline. You arrive at the falls at the lower end, and it is very rare to see such a powerful waterfall from this angle. This is one of south iceland's best photo opportunities and it may be tempting to take a shower, but the weight of water would probably be fatal.

Drive on instead to the thermal swimming pool at **Seljavellir** (turn off at 609km/378 miles). You can sit in a 'hot pot' here and enjoy the mountain panorama.

★**Seljalandsfoss** (628km/390 miles) provides another encounter with water. It is possible here to follow the waterfall along a downhill path. Soon after you will cross the **Markarfljót** glacial river on a new bridge. This watercourse carries meltwater from the Eyjafjallajökull and Mýrdalsjökull glaciers down to the sea.

WOODLAND WALKS

Some way inland in the rain shadow of Eyjafjallajökull is the peaceful woodland area of the ★★**Þórsmörk Valley**. Surrounded by a rugged glacier backdrop, it is one of the most popular destinations on the highland fringes and has several mountain cabins and campsites.

A variety of walking tours start here. One undemanding option is an afternoon walk through the nearby woods. For those seeking something a little more challenging, try a mountain walk southwards to the coast near Skógar.

Dedicated trekkers might prefer to investigate a four-day hike to **Landmannalaugar**. Þórsmörk can be reached only in a large four-wheel-drive vehicle or as part of a bus trip from **Hvolsvöllur** (650km/404 miles), which marks the beginning of the more densely populated region of Iceland. Some of the farmhouse names have connections with the medieval sagas, in particular the Njálssaga. The **Saga Centre** (May–September, Monday–Friday 9am–6pm, Saturday–Sunday 10am–6pm; www.njala.is) with its accessible exhibition is signposted on the main road.

Selfoss (700km/435 miles) has a population of about 6,000 and is the largest inland town in Iceland. It occupies an important position in the road network of southwest Iceland and is the centre of a predominantly agricultural region. The main employer in the town is one of northern Europe's largest dairies.

EDEN GREENHOUSE

The greenhouse town of **Hveragerði** (712km/442 miles) has unique expertise in using geothermal energy to overcome the harsh North Atlantic climate. Thanks to hot water flowing from underground spring, exotic flowers, fruit and other plants are cultivated here under glass to meet the Icelanders' demand for tomatoes, cucumbers and bananas. Some of the greenhouses sell their products to the passing public at reasonable prices.

Practically every coach stops at the ★**Eden** greenhouse (Austurmörk 25, tel: 483 4900). The attractions here are the greenhouse, a huge souvenir shop and a café that serves rather pricey snacks under palm trees.

The Ring Road gradually snakes its way up to **Hellisheiði** and, after crossing a 1,000-year-old lava plateau, finally arrives in **Reykjavík** (750km/466 miles).

Star Attraction
● **Skógafoss**

Yule Lads
Just north of Hveragerði are the hot springs of Grýla, named after a wicked ogress with a penchant for devouring small children. She had thirteen sons – Iceland's Yule Lads, who creep down from the hills one at a time from 13 days before Christmas until Christmas Eve to cause mischief to decent folk. Their malice has been downgraded over the years: once they were feared by children, now they leave little presents for them – if they've been well behaved.

Iceland's edible berries: crowberries and blueberries

Map pages 40-1

THE WESTMAN ISLANDS

The Westman archipelago (Vestmannaeyjar), comprising 15 islands and about 30 skerries and rocks, was formed during the past 10,000 to 20,000 years on what is one of the most volcanically active belts in the world. It was basically a case of one eruption equals one island (the most recent being Surtsey, which emerged in 1963). There is only one exception – the inhabited ★★**Heimaey** island, which was formed from a series of eruptions.

CRISIS ON HEIMAEY

On 23 January 1973, without any warning, a new volcano, later to be christened Eldfell or 'Fire Mountain', erupted on the eastern side of the Heimaey town. Lava and ash buried 400 houses for ever, but the 6,000 inhabitants of Heimaey were safely evacuated during the night. Because there had been a storm the day before, the island's fishing fleet was at anchor in harbour and fortuitously the crews were on hand to rescue all the islanders from the fiery explosion without any loss of life.

Below: molten lava
Bottom: some of the 1973 damage

This eruption lasted for about six months, during which time volunteers tried to protect house contents from the lava and the constant showers of ash. At one point a lava flow threatened to destroy the town's natural harbour, an important part of the fishing community's livelihood. In desperation, helpers showered millions and millions of litres of seawater over the advancing river of molten lava and, despite all predictions to the contrary, they managed to bring the flow to a standstill and, remarkably, in such a way that the harbour entrance is now better protected than it was before.

The 5,000 inhabitants of the Heimaey fishing community make up less than two percent of the Icelandic population, yet they account for some 12 percent of their country's exports.

The residents of Heimaey now live only a few metres from the wall of lava, a tourist attraction that is best viewed from Kirkjuvegur and Heimagata. With few cars on the island, the streets are empty and peaceful. The **Folk Museum** has a well organised set of relics, model ships and photographs. recording life on the island.

Star Attraction
● Heimaey Island

MARINE LIFE

On the island's shores the sea has created steep cliffs and spectacular caves. Millions of sea birds nest here, including countless puffins, which form part of the Westman Islanders' diet, along with guillemots and the eggs of the storm petrel, as well as sea grass.

Heimaey's **Aquarium and Natural History Museum** (open 1 May–1 September, daily 11am–5pm, October–April, Saturday and Sunday 3–5pm) has an interesting display of stuffed birds, with the emphasis on those species that nest on the island. Large tanks house an interesting collection of fish found around the islands, including the strange-looking Icelandic cod and catfish.

In September 1998 the island welcomed a new guest: Keikó, the killer whale, star of the Hollywood film *Free Willy*, and for many years a prisoner in an American oceanarium. He was brought here prior to being released in the North Atlantic. Sadly, however, after moving on to Norway, Keikó died of pneumonia in 2003.

> **Surviving disaster**
> The inhabitants of Heimaey are well acquainted with catastrophe. Epidemics wracked the island in the 17th and 18th centuries; the 1783 eruption of Laki on the mainland killed off all the fish around the islands, forcing the inhabitants to live on sea birds; and numerous fishing accidents have taken a terrible toll on the population. All of this may have accounted for their famous sangfroid in the face of the 1973 volcanic eruption.

Westman Islands

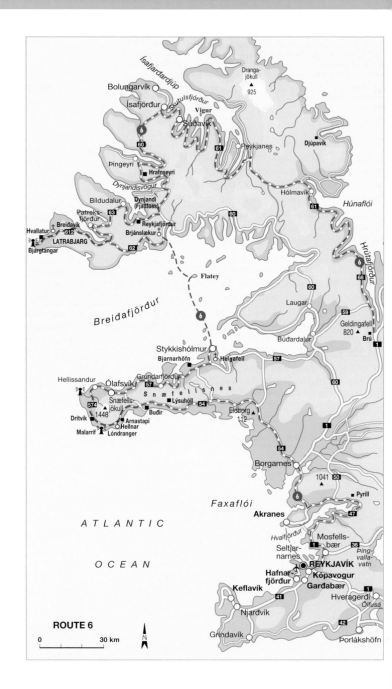

ROUTE 6

0 _____ 30 km

6: Snæfellsnes and the Westfjords

Reykjavík – Snæfellsjökull – Stykkishólmur – Flatey – Látrabjarg – Ísafjörður – Brú (1,031km/ 640 miles)

Star Attraction
● Borgarnes

This route goes round the tip of the Snæfellsnes peninsula, where you will see one of the finest mountains in the world, the ice-capped Snæfell-sjökull volcano which, at 1,446 metres (4,743 ft), dominates the countryside. From Stykkishólmur, an attractive little town, a ferry sails through the Breiðafjörður islands to the largely unexplored Westfjords. While very popular with bird enthusiasts, the region is also essential viewing for lovers of remote, spectacular landscapes.

Out of the land mass – one of the oldest in Iceland – natural forces have forged a series of fjords – fingers of water that cut deep into the peninsula. Beyond the narrow, thinly populated coastal strip, steep slopes ascend to lonely mountain ridges and marshy plateaux. Impressive cliffs, long stretches of sandy beaches, magnificent waterfalls, a few hot springs and one glacier reveal the full splendour of the diverse landscape typical of Iceland.

Travelling in the northwest requires more time than other regions, partly because the weather can be very unpredictable. You should allow three days for this route – although there are enough sights to keep most travellers occupied for a week. The section around Snæfellsjökull can be covered in a day, albeit a strenuous one, from Reykjavík.

Below: exploring Snæfellsnes
Bottom: delicate flora

BORGANES

Leave **Reykjavík** on the northern Ring Road. The Hvalfjörður tunnel (toll: ISK 1,000), opened in 1998, saves about 50km (30 miles) or about an hour of driving along winding roads beside the fjord. It is, nevertheless, worth the effort if the weather is fine *(see page 28)*. All distances for Route 7 include the detour around the fjord.
★★**Borgarnes** (pop. 2,000; 117km/73 miles) is one of the most important towns in western Ice-

Map on page 76

Reykholt

Some 36km (22 miles) east of Borgarnes lies the tiny hamlet of Reykholt, the home of Snorri Sturluson, who was murdered on the orders of the King of Norway in 1241. The farmstead is long gone, but a hot pool remains where the scholar and chieftain once bathed. The village also has a modern sculpture of Snorri, a church and a research centre.

Basalt columns on Snæfellsnes

land and a hub for traffic on the Snæfellsnes peninsula and the Westfjords. It occupies a special place among Iceland's towns – it is situated beside the sea but, unusually, fishing plays no part in the local economy.

The town's attraction for tourists lies in its association with figures from the Icelandic sagas, in particular the famous *Egils Saga*. Skallagrímur Kveldúlfsson, the first settler in the region and father of the saga hero, Egill Skallagrímsson, is said to be buried in a small park in the town centre, together with Böðvar, his grandson. Just north of the town, where paved Highway 54 branches off the Ring Road towards Snæfellsnes, lies **Borg á Myrum** farmhouse, where the two lived during the 10th century. Some 200 years later, Egill's descendant, the diplomat and scholar Snorri Sturluson, assumed to be the writer of the *Egils Saga*, married into the Borg family.

THE SNÆFELLSNES PENINSULA

The **Snæfellsnes peninsula** is not one of Iceland's most active volcanic zones, but the first summit you will see (152km/94 miles) is the **Eldborg** volcano or Fire Fort. This very evenly formed crater rises about 60m (200ft) from a field of lava. Huge basalt columns on the **Gerðuberg** (164km/102 miles), visible from the road to the Höfði farmhouse, are reminders of earlier volcanic activity. If you follow this road northwards for about 5km (3 miles) as far as an overgrown lava field, you will discover **Rauðamelsökelda** spring (10 minutes' walk). The carbonated flow tastes much better than any bottled mineral water.

Water from a warm spring is used for the hot pots at the swimming pool in **Lýsuhóll** school and community centre (212km/132 miles).

On a clear day, the ice-capped ★★ **Snæfellsjökull** volcano, with two other summits close by (1,442m/4,730ft and 1,446m/4,744ft), dominates the skyline. Jules Verne took Snæfellsjökull as the starting point for the heroic adventures he described in *Journey to the Centre of the Earth*, and Iceland's Nobel prize winner for literature,

Halldór Laxness *(see page 99)*, chose to use the volcano as the backdrop for his novel *Under the Glacier*, an acerbic attack on the Church.

Star Attraction
● Snæfellsjökull

THE GLACIER SUMMIT

The glacier can be approached from several directions: the summit is four to five hours' walk from Arnarstapi. A ski lift goes to the top at weekends in winter. From Ólafsvík, north of the glacier, it is possible to drive part of the way and then walk on – again, a four- to five-hour hike to the summit. While the highest of the three mountain peaks is difficult to scale without special climbing gear, the walk up the glacier itself is fairly easy. In summer, however, crevasses open in the ice, so a guided walk is recommended (available from Ólafsvík).

*Below: church at Búðir
Bottom: Snæfellsjökull*

Route 6 now follows coastal highway 574 around Snæfellsjökull. **Búðir**, once an important fishing centre, became better known for a pleasant hotel of the same name. After a fire in 2001 the hotel has been carefully restored and has reopened. Only a few metres away, past an attractive timber church and a small cemetery, lies an idyllic beach, where the sand dunes contrast strikingly with the pitch black lava rock. When the weather is fine, the snow-covered Snæfellsjökull glacier makes a striking backdrop.

Map
on page
76

Approaching Snæfellsjökull, you will pass large farmhouses dotted along the flat strip of land between the mountain slopes and the shoreline. A four-wheel-drive vehicle is needed to approach the volcano's east flank via track F570, but it is possible to take an ordinary car the few hundred metres to ★ **Sönghellir** cave. Do bear in mind that a guide with experience of glaciers is an essential companion and all the necessary safety measures must be taken. Some fatal accidents have occurred on Snæfellsjökull because the area's dangers have been underestimated. Guided tours on the glacier are organised from Arnastapi and Ólafsvík *(see page 82)*.

Sönghellir cave
Sönghellir echo or song cave has remarkable acoustics and a huge stone arch. It is also the starting point for some fine glacier walks.

Basalt bridge at Arnastapi

Basalt Coastline

★★ **Arnastapi** (238km/148 miles) is the tourist gateway to Snæfellsjökull, and is also famous for its birdlife and its spectacular coastline formations of basalt caves and bridges. The distinctive symbol for this settlement is the huge stone monument to Bárður Snæfellsás, a character from the medieval sagas.

The basalt coast is just as impressive by the next village, **Hellnar**, some 2km (1¼ miles) from the main road. Make a point of exploring the sea-level *Baðstofa* (Bathroom Cave), where bizarre effects of light and colour can be seen. The rocks beside the two rock pillars of **Lóndrangar** (246km/152 miles) are among the best vantage points in the whole of Iceland for observing sea birds.

Snæfellsjökull shows its best face over the next few kilometres, particularly on summer evenings. Solidified lava flows formed many thousands of years ago have taken on weird and wonderful shapes. The volcano beneath the glacier cap has never erupted during the human history of Iceland, but it is not considered extinct.

After 250km (155 miles) a road branches off to the sea. It is a half-hour walk from the end to the former fishing village of **Dritvík**. Abandoned many years ago, there is now nothing left but wilderness, although it is still possible to pick out some foundation walls. If the spectacular lava

coast is bathed in the golden evening sunlight,
then the atmosphere is idyllic; when the harsh
west wind blows, however, this is a raw and inhospitable place.

The road steers a course between glacier and
sea through fields of lava of varying ages. Smallish craters can be spotted from time to time. The
first sign of habitation is the tallest structure in
Iceland, the 412-m (1,351-ft) high transmitter
mast at **Gufuskálar** (275km/171 miles).

SEAFARING TRADITION

A little further on, on the edge of **Hellissandur**
(278km/173 miles), is a small folk museum that
charts the history of fishing and seafaring in the
region. When fishermen had only small flat-bot-
tomed rowing boats and an auxiliary sail, it was
important that the men lived near their fishing
grounds. There was no need for a harbour. All
they required was a sandy beach.

During the season several hundred fishermen
lived in places like Dritvík. Even though they
fished the nearby waters, the work was very
demanding. Before throwing out their nets the
men often had to row hard for four to five hours
and a fishing expedition could take up a whole
day. If the catches were good, the men would go
out to sea again, sometimes making two, three
or even four trips one after the other.

Star Attraction
● Arnastapi

*Below: monument to
Bárður Snæfellsás
Bottom: Church at
Hellissandur*

Map
on page
76

Ólafsvík
Ólafsvík is one of the larger communities on the peninsula and it is also Iceland's oldest-established trading town, granted its charter in 1687. The town offers a guesthouse and restaurants, a swimming pool and golf course.

Stykkishólmur

TEST OF STRENGTH

Only fit men could do this work. What separated the men from the boys were the lifting stones that can still be seen in Djúpalón bay near Dritvík and in other places. To secure a place on one of the fishing boats, a man had to lift the 50kg (100lb) *hálfdrættinger* stone. Professional fishermen could lift the 140-kg (300-lb) *hálfsterkur* and many even managed to lift the 155-kg (350-lb) *fullsterkur* a metre above the ground.

Commercial fishing started in Iceland in the 16th century. The abandoned settlements on the west coast of Snæfellsnes enjoyed their best years in the 17th and 18th centuries. With the arrival of enclosed sailing boats in the mid-19th century, followed by the steam-driven trawlers from 1906 onwards, deepwater harbours were necessary and at that time there were none in this part of Iceland.

WHALEWATCHING IN ÓLAFSVIK

The harbour in **Ólafsvík** keeps many of the 1,200-plus inhabitants in work (288km/179 miles), but proximity to Snæfellsjökull also boosts income from tourism. A modern church and a 19th-century warehouse, now home to the tourist office and local museum, are worth investigating.

Two catamarans, *Brimrún* and *Særún*, based in Ólafsvík, provide some of Iceland's best ★★ **whalewatching** off the Snæfellsnes peninsula (June–mid-August, once daily, up to 7 hours; about ISK 13,000). The huge mammals, mainly blue whales up to 190 tonnes in weight and 34m (110ft) long, are sighted on nearly all trips; humpback whales can also sometimes be spotted.

ANCIENT LAVA FIELD

Route 6 follows Highway 57 eastwards along the north coast of the Snæfellsnes peninsula. The pyramid-shaped **Kirkjufell** (463m/1,520ft) near **Grundarfjörður** (316km/196 miles) is one of the most beautiful and most striking mountains in Iceland. The road hugs the coastline for a while and then follows a new course past the legendary

Berserkjahraun, a lava field at least 4,000 years old. In the Saga Age 'berserks' were wild and burly warriors who sought to boost their strength in battle by wearing animal furs. The Berserk-jahraun is named after two such fighting men. According to the Eyrbyggjasaga, a farmer enlisted the two men to clear a path through the lava to his brother's farm, but instead of paying them, the farmer killed them. They were apparently buried in a deep pit in the Berserkjahraun beside the path that they had hewn.

The destination for the path was **Bjarnarhöfn** farm by the sea. The owner now uses it as a base for shark fishing. Visitors to the farm can observe the traditional methods of shark processing and even sample some of the meat (tel: 438 1581).

At the foot of the colourful rhyolite **Drápuhlíðarfjall** peak (353km/219 miles), the result of volcanic activity, a road forks off to the left to Stykkishólmur. This passes the sacred ★★**Mount Helgafell** (Holy Mountain; 73m/240ft), a shrine to Thor in pagan times, later the site of an Augustinian monastery, and an important site in the Icelandic sagas.

Star Attractions
- **Mount Helgafell**
- **Whalewatching**

STYKKISHÓLMUR

The futuristic **church** in one of Iceland's most delightful towns (363km/226 miles) dominates the area. Strangely, the bell-tower, now a sym-

Below and bottom:
Stykkishólmur

Map on page 76

Mount Helgafell
Local folklore holds that first-time climbers of the mountain will have three wishes come true, provided a few conditions are observed: you must not look back or speak on the way; you must make your wishes facing east; you must not tell anyone what they are; and only benevolent wishes are allowed. Even if your wishes are not granted, Helgafell is well worth climbing to enjoy the spectacular views over Breiðafjörður bay.

Stone figure guarding the route to Patreksfjörður

bol for ★ **Stykkishólmur**, is structurally too weak for any bells. Was this an attempt by government-inspired Protestants to break the dominance of the Dutch-run Catholic convent? The monastery complex, built in 1936 and also home to the regional hospital, dominates the port area. There are some stunning views from the island of **Súgandisey** – accessible via a causeway from the harbour – over the 3,000-plus islands, islets and rocks in Breiðafjörður and also over the mountain panorama behind Stykkishólmur. It is definitely worth making the short walk – on light summer evenings this is a truly romantic spot.

Many of the older buildings in the harbour area have been preserved. The beautifully restored **Norwegian House**, for example, imported in kit form from Norway and built in 1828, was the first two-storey private dwelling on Iceland. It is now home to the **Byggðasafn Snæfellinga og Hnappdœla** regional museum (Hafnargata 5, tel: 438 1640; June–August, daily 11am–5pm). The library makes a good vantage point for views over the town centre and harbour.

Flatey Island

The journey by ferry through the labyrinth of islands in ★ **Breiðafjörður** is one of the highlights of this tour of western Iceland. The *Baldur* makes one or two sailings per day, depending on the time of year, from Stykkishólmur to Brjánslækur.

The boat stops off at the island of ★★ **Flatey**, the site of a 12th-century monastery and a major cultural centre until the 1800s. If the weather is fine, then it is a good idea to catch the morning ferry and stop over until the afternoon ferry arrives. As Flatey is a motor vehicle-free zone, you will have to leave your vehicle on the ferry anyway. It is then driven on to land by the crew in Brjánslækur and can be collected later.

Flatey is a delight, a perfectly preserved example of what an Icelandic village used to be. Barely a handful of people live here all year round, but during the summer months the population swells to several hundred when former islanders or their families return to their roots and renovate their ancestors' houses.

The bird life on Flatey and the surrounding skerries is a source of fascination for both ornithologists and laymen. Excursions for short-stay visitors can be booked on the *Baldur*. If you are intending to stay longer on the island, check carefully about the availability of provisions.

EUROPE'S MOST WESTERLY POINT

From the landing stage at **Brjánslækur** (camp-site nearby), this route will take you to the west-ernmost point in Europe. First you must cross the 400-m (1,300-ft) high **Kleifaheiði** to reach **Patreksfjörður**. Be prepared for a bit of a fright if you are travelling in the mist, as a stone fig-ure with a stern expression looks down on trav-ellers from the roadside. Road builders erected this monument in memory of their predecessors.

At the mouth of Patreksfjörður (405km/252 miles), Highway 612 branches off to Látrabjarg. As a symbol of progress, Iceland's first steel trawler stands in a roadside field.

The ★ **Folk Museum** in **Hnjótur** (429km/267 miles) is packed full of exhibits documenting the history of fishing, seafaring and aviation in the region. In front of the building stands a replica of a Viking ship, a Russian biplane and an

Star Attractions
- **Mount Helgafell**
- **Flatey Island**

Below: birdwatching at Látrabjarg
Bottom: puffins

Map on page 76

American DC3 once stationed at Keflavík.

Breiðavík, once a busy fishing harbour consists of a small church and an old boarding school. There is accommodation and a weekly bus service to Látrabjarg cliffs for tourists here and it is worth taking a stroll along the lovely sandy beach. The neighbouring village of **Hvallátur** also used to be a thriving fishing port. Look for the heavy lifting stones by the shore. Recruits for fishing expeditions would have been asked to lift them by their masters as a test of strength *(see page 82)*.

A narrow road runs from here to the westernmost point in Europe, **Bjargtangar**, one of the ★★**Látrabjarg** cliffs (455km/283 miles). Countless sea birds nest on these 14-km (9-mile) long and up to 444-m (1,456-m) high, often vertical, basalt rocks, probably the most dramatic section of the Icelandic coastline.

TEEMING BIRDLIFE

Puffins can often be seen in the carpark only a few metres from the lighthouse; these attractive creatures are very happy to be photographed. If you take a walk along the cliff top, you can watch fulmars dancing above the precipice. Perched on the ledges lower down are guillemots and razorbills – the world's largest population of this species

Below: Dynjandi waterfall
Bottom: Hnífsdalur, on the coast north of Ísafjörður

make their home on this headland. Look down over the rock face and you will see the shags watching the shoreline from the front row.

Southeast of Látrabjarg is Iceland's most magnificent stretch of golden sand, Rauðasandur.

Star Attraction
● **Látrabjarg cliffs**

SMOKY FJORD

You must now retrace your steps along Highway 62 (505km/313 miles). Under a local government reorganisation scheme, the port of **Patreksfjörður** (517km/321 miles) has merged with the neighbouring settlements as far as Bíldudalur (545km/339 miles) to create the community of **Vesturbyggð**. The northern section of this municipality lies beside one of the arms of the vast **Arnarfjörður**, named after Örn, an early settler in the region.

Reykjafjörður (563km/350 miles), or Smoky Fjord, has hot springs and it is well worth relaxing for a while in the warm roadside pool to summon up strength for the arduous journey ahead. Up in the mountains you will join Highway 60 (580km/360 miles), which starts at the ferry terminal in Brjánslækur *(see page 85)*, from here only 14km (9 miles) away; the circuit via Látrabjarg involves a detour of 217km (134 miles).

On the bleak and remote Dynjandisheiði moor, the road reaches an altitude of 500m (1,600ft) before winding its lonely way down to **Dynjandisvogur** bay.

After 602km (374 miles) it is worth pulling up to admire one of Iceland's finest waterfalls, ★ **Dynjandi**, also known as Fjallfoss, which is situated a few hundred metres from the road. The water tumbles across a broad face down almost 100m (330ft) over curving basalt steps.

The 300 inhabitants of **Þingeyri** (640km/398 miles) live mainly from fishing, but the village used to be a trading post and Hanseatic merchants were once active here. Continue along this road and you will come to one of Iceland's most important road-building projects. A three-way tunnel, almost 9km (5 miles) in length, connects Flateyri and Suðureyri with the Westfjords capital of

> **Rescue operation**
> When the British trawler *Dhoon* ran aground below the Látrabjarg cliffs in the winter of 1947, a remarkable rescue operation by the local farmers saved all 12 crew members. Lowering themselves by ropes as if they were collecting eggs, the farmers hauled the exhausted men up the 200-metre (650-ft) cliff-face to safety.

Jón Sigurdsson, leader of the Independence Movement, was born at Hrafnseyri near Dynjandi

Map on page 76

Hrafnseyri
After Dynjandi, just before the road turns away from the coast towards the next climb, you will pass the Hrafnseyri vicarage (622km/386 miles). It has been in existence since Viking times and was the birthplace of one of Iceland's most celebrated figures, Jón Sigurðsson. The museum and memorial recall the life of this tireless fighter for Icelandic independence. Independence Day celebrations are held here on 17 June, Jón's birthday.

Ísafjörður. Mountain bikers and walkers may prefer to take the old route over the mountains, if they wish to avoid the exhaust gases in the tunnel. If the weather is fine, they will be rewarded with some stunning views.

MEDIEVAL TRADING CENTRE

The area's only town of any significant size, ★★ **Ísafjörður** (690km/429 miles) can trace its history back to Iceland's Settlement. It was on this peninsula, where the old town centre is located, that the first settler, Helgi Hrólfsson, took land, naming the fjord where he built his farmhouse **Skutulsfjörður** or 'Harpoon Fjord', because he found an old harpoon on the beach.

Ísafjörður has been the main trading centre for the region since the late Middle Ages, initially under the control of Hanseatic traders, later under the Danish Trade Monopoly. In 1786 Ísafjörður obtained the status of an official trading post, one of only six in the country. At the end of the 19th century, the largest private trading company in Iceland at that time was based here, but during the 1920s it was taken over by a co-operative.

Today, a stroll through the old town is an unforgettable walk through the past. A cluster of houses on the southern side of the Eyri peninsula date from the 18th century, when the Danes held sway.

Rural church in the Westfjords

The ★ **West Fjords Maritime Museum**
(Suðurtangi; June–mid-September, Tuesday–
Sunday 1–5pm) houses an interesting collection
of fishing paraphernalia dedicated to maritime
travel, trade and fishing.

Ísafjörður outgrew the Eyri peninsula long ago
and now extends along the northwest shores of
Skutulsfjörður. The town's leisure area is situated
to the northwest in the valleys that run into the
end of the fjord. There are many summer homes,
a campsite in **Tungudal** and a winter sports centre in **Seljalandsdal**. Every year over the Easter
week a skiing and folk festival is held in the town.
The island of ★ **Vigur** is a popular destination
for boat trips, which focus on the bird life and a
primitive farmhouse possessing Iceland's only
surviving windmill.

Below: Ísafjörður local
Bottom: lighthouse
on Reykjanes

The town itself provides a good vantage point
for views over the mouth of the Ísafjarðardjúp
fjord. There is also an interesting folk museum
with a replica of the Ósvör fishing base, which
dates from the time when fishermen used rowing boats. **Gullauga Goldsmiths**, at Hafnarstræti
4, sell gold and stone pieces at designer prices.
If you are interested in buying locally produced
handicrafts directly from the makers, take the trip
to **Bolungarvík** (Drymla, Skólastigur 3–5), 15km
(9 miles) to the north. Enquire at the tourist information office for opening times.

SMOKY PENINSULA

You will be able to enjoy the full splendour of the
fjords as you continue southwards beside **Ísafjarðardjúp**. As the crow flies, it is only 40km (25
miles) to the end of the fjord system; but by road
the journey is 175km (108 miles). The only major
settlement on this section is **Súðavík**. The centre of the village (pop. 200) was devastated by
an avalanche during snowstorms in 1995 *(see
page 19)*.

At the end of the southernmost finger of land
jutting out into this fjord system lies **Reykjanes**
or 'Smoky Peninsula' (17km/10 miles from the
main road). The thermal spring water is used for

Map on page 76

Relaxing soak
At the end of this long journey, travellers can recover from their exertions in one of Iceland's most remote swimming pools. Only a stone's throw from the icy North Atlantic, the Krossneslaug is supplied by the pleasantly warm water that flows from a hot spring.

Hrútafjörður

a swimming pool and sauna at a former school complex, now converted into a hotel and a restaurant, which stays open all year.

After the journey around Ísafjörður, Highway 61 crosses the **Steingrímsfjarðarheiði** plateau, an almost Arctic moraine landscape. Until well into the first half of the 19th century, ice from the Drangajökull glacier, now retreated northwards, covered this inhospitable terrain.

STRANDIR COAST

By **Steingrímsfjörður**, Highway 643 branches off Route 6 to the sparsely populated and desolate **Strandir coast** in the north, a 102-km (63-mile) long cul-de-sac that reaches into an area which sees very little in the way of tourism. The journey is a veritable feast for the eyes. Seals can often be seen basking by the shore.

Djúpavík, a once-bustling herring station, is now virtually abandoned save for its wonderfully situated **Hótel Djúpavík**, which provided lodgings for the women who toiled in the herring factory here.

Hólmavík (pop. 350) is the only town of any size on the Strandir coast. Amenities for tourists include an information office (summer, tel: 451 3510) where local handicrafts are sold. There is also a petrol station with a cafeteria and supermarket across the road.

The route now runs southwards past **Húnaflói** bay and its continuation **Hrútafjörður**. You will see an increasing number of farmhouses, even the occasional photogenic church, with **Prestbakki** (1,005km/624 miles) probably the most attractive. On those stretches where the road runs alongside the shore, it will become apparent that the local farmers run a profitable sideline processing driftwood. Arctic sea currents from Siberia regularly deliver large consignments of tree trunks free of charge.

Close to **Brú** (1,031km/640 miles) the route finally meets up with the Ring Road again. It is 202km (125 miles) to Reykjavík, 230km (143 miles) to Akureyri.

7: The Central Highlands

**The Kjölur Route (F35): Gullfoss – Hveravellir
– Blöndudalur (180km/111 miles)**
**The Sprengisandur Route (F26): Sigalda –
Sprengisandur – Goðafoss (234km/145 miles)**

Central Iceland offers a taste of adventure. It is
a bleak and barren landscape like no other in
Europe. Some of the smaller rivers have to be
forded and tracks are often barely identifiable as
they pass through seemingly endless fields of
loose gravel. The appeal of the Icelandic highlands lies in its boundless dimensions. Glaciers
and mountains on the horizon provide constant
visual delights.

Both of these highland tracks are popular and
easy one-day excursions from the capital, but it
is better to arrange accommodation for an
overnight stay, perhaps in the hiking clubs' mountain cabins.

The highland tracks are open to traffic only
when they have firmed up after the snow has
melted in late spring. If you intend to cross the
highland plain in your own vehicle or by bus, do
not arrive before the middle of July as the tracks
may not be open. The dates given here are based
on average values. More details are available from
the website www.vegag.is.

*Below: cauldron on the
Kjölur plateau*
*Bottom: bathing in a
natural thermal pool*

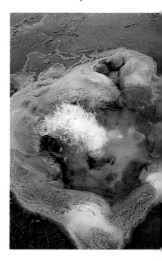

Map on pages 40–1

Scheduled buses run cross-country between Reykjavík and Akureyri and between Reykjavík and Mývatn.

THE KJÖLUR ROUTE

> **The Kjölur route**
> This route, often closed by snow and ice until well into the summer, is an ancient track, which was used during the Middle Ages for driving cattle as it passes through a number of grazing meadows. Legend has it that one year four shepherds and their sheep perished in a storm as they crossed the mountains. Their bones were found years later. The hill near the disaster was named Beinahóll or 'Bone Hill'.

The Kjölur route, based on an ancient byway used in Saga times, is one of the main routes across the interior, passing between the Langjökull and Hofsjökull icecaps. A four-wheel drive is advisable but other vehicles are seen on the main track which begins at the majestic ★★ **Gullfoss** waterfall in the Southwest (Route 2; *see page 37*) and runs northwards to the **Blöndudalur** valley. The first part of the journey, to the hot springs of Hveravellir, is on a road of gravel, stones and rock, with the occasional small river to be forded. Beyond Hveravellir, the route deteriorates as the track becomes muddy with several extended river crossings. In comparison with other routes across the interior, the Kjölur is relatively busy during the summer and could be tackled in a day.

The track is named after the 700-m (2,300-ft) high **Kjölur** plateau, set between the Langjökull and Hofsjökull glaciers, whose two similar-sized ice-caps dominate the surrounding landscape.

The steamy oasis of Hveravellir

Start this tour at **Gullfoss**. The **Hvítá** river, the power behind this spectacular waterfall, flows out

of ★★ **Hvítárvatn**, a glacial lake at the foot of **Langjökull** icecap. It is possible to see the lake and its glacial spurs, which extend up to its shores, from the main route and also the somewhat rougher parallel section, which branches off after **Hvítar bridge** (34km/21 miles).

The main route soon reaches its highest point (just over 670m/2,200ft), where a memorial stone (74km/45 miles) has successfully withstood the harshest of weather conditions. This monument, which also serves as a viewing point, commemorates the achievements of Geir Zoëga, an engineer who was for many years in charge of building Iceland's roads.

HVERAVELLIR

At the centre of the Kjölur plateau it is easy for travellers to forget the inhospitable climate. ★★ **Hveravellir** geothermal area offers hot springs, and even a hot pool for a relaxing soak.

The benefits of this oasis were appreciated in the 18th century. Fjalla Eyvindur and his wife Halla endured a whole winter up here in hiding. This notorious pair of bandits spent much of their life on the run from the authorities. A modest shelter made out of stone and the hot spring that Eyvindur converted into a cooking pot are among the few man-made sights in this barren terrain.

The northern section is less attractive, as for a long way the route follows a new track through the reservoir basin created for **Blönduvirkjun** hydro-electric power station (161km/100 miles). After crossing the **Blanda** river (180km/112 miles) at about halfway between Blönduós and Varmahlíð *(see page 45)*, you will reach the **Blöndudalur** and then link up with Route 3.

THE SPRENGISANDUR ROUTE F26

The Sprengisandur Route usually opens at the beginning of July and two alternative routes, which are even tougher, the F821 to Akureyri and the F752 to Varmahlíð, are accessible about two weeks later.

Star Attraction
● Hvítárvatn

Below: vent at Hveravellir
Bottom: lichens

Map on pages 40–1

Keeping warm

At Nýidalur, close to the geographical centre of Iceland, stand several huts – invariably a welcome sight. There is a small campsite on the only patch of green in the area, but even in the middle of summer high winds and near-freezing temperatures make camping a desperate option. The better choice is to stay in the huts which offer both warmth and hospitality. Wardened during the summer months, the atmosphere inside these huts is always congenial, with travellers swapping tales and sharing food.

Aldeyjarfoss

This section of road has had a bad reputation since the Middle Ages – the capricious weather, robbers and evil spirits all making for a hazardous journey. The *Sprengisandur song*, which tells of a rider's fears of evil forces as he follows the track, is one of the most popular folk songs in Iceland and is often sung when people get together in the evenings.

To reach the starting point for this tour, you will probably have to follow Route 2 *(see page 35)* as far as Þjórsárdalur. The **Sigalda power station** is the latest of three high-output hydro-electric stations that harness the currents of the Þjórsá and Tungnaá rivers, which generate electricity for the Reykjavík area as well as the aluminium smelter in Straumsvík.

The route then runs alongside the western shores of **Þórisvatn**. For the benefit of the power station, this lake has been enlarged from its natural size of about 70 sq. km (27 sq. miles) to almost 90 sq. km (34 sq. miles), making it the largest lake in Iceland. After crossing the **Kaldakvísl bridge** (78km/48 miles) the road becomes more of a track, not all of the rivers and streams are bridged and the vegetation becomes noticeably more sparse.

The green **Nýidalur** (150km/93 miles) is a good starting point for hiking tours, some of which can reach to the edge of the smallish **Tungnafellsjökull** glacier. This oasis marks the start of the ★**Sprengisandur**, an expanse of moorland some 200 sq. km (75 sq. miles) in area and 700–800m (2,300–2,600ft) high.

ALDEYJARFOSS

The track passes through long sections of monotonous scree landscape. Just before **Mýri** farmhouse (246km/153 miles) a side road branches off to ★★**Aldeyjarfoss**, one of the finest waterfalls in Iceland. The **Skjálfandafljót** glacial river cascades 20m (65ft) down a layer of basalt columns. Further north it provides the flow for the ★**Goðafoss** (234km/145 miles) on Route 4 *(see page 40)*.

8: Askja and Kverkjökull

Hrossaborg – Herðubreið – Askja – Kverkfjöll – Möðrudalur (272km/169 miles)

In the northeast, on both sides of the Jökulsá á Fjöllum, the highland area is criss-crossed by a network of tracks only negotiable by four-wheel drive vehicles. Up-to-date maps are essential. This route follows tracks F88 as well as F910, F902 and F903. They usually open between the middle and end of June. Allow at least two if not three days for this tour.

Three times a week in July and August day trips run to Askja from Mývatn. And 3-day Ice and Fire expeditions run along Route 7 but in the opposite direction. Ask at tourist information offices or Destination Iceland *(see page 110)*.

*Below: taking in the views
Bottom: steaming glacier at the edge of the Kverkfjöll*

QUEEN OF THE ICELANDIC MOUNTAINS

Leave the Ring Road 7km (4 miles) to the west of Grímsstaðir *(see Route 4 on page 54)* by the **Hrossaborg** crater. Apart from the challenges presented by lava fields and two sizeable fords, the first hour's driving through the **Ódáðahraun** wastes would be fairly monotonous were it not for the views of the ever-present ★★ **Herðubreið**, the 'Queen of the Icelandic mountains'.

Map on pages 40–1

Desert wildlife
Only the hardiest plants and animals survive in this part of Iceland. The ancient and twisted frames of dwarf willow are testimony to the harshness of the environment. Other forms of life can be spotted by careful observers: among the dark gravel lie balls of primordial-looking grey lichens, while under stones protected from the wind sit small brown moths, barely moving, the only visible sign of animal life.

This 1,682-m/5,518-ft high table volcano began to form sub-glacially during the last Ice Age. Wherever the ejected lava came into contact with ice and meltwater, it left behind on the steep mountain slopes a loose and porous material that is difficult to climb. Only when the ice-cap had pushed about 900m/3,000ft above the surrounding terrain did it form itself into a basalt plateau, dominated by a 150 m/ 500-ft high volcanic cone with its own crater.

OASIS IN THE DESERT

★ **Herðubreiðarlindir** (60km/37 miles) lies at the foot of Herðubreið, and is an oasis of wild flowers and water springs. Over 100 plant species have been identified here: you will have to seek out the small, bright blue mountain gentian, whereas it is hard to miss the violet Arctic fireweed and the huge clumps of angelica. Another of the shelters built by the outlaw, Fjalla Eyvindur (*see page 93*), can be found here.

The next few miles of track pass through a barren lava field scattered with bright chunks of buoyant pumice stone. It was here that NASA astronauts rehearsed their first steps on the moon. Nowhere else on earth has ground conditions so similar to those on the moon.

Smoking landscape

Beside ★ **Drekagil** (90km/56 miles) – the

Dragon's Gorge – lies the **Dyngjufjöll** volcanic massif, better known as ★ **Askja**, although this name strictly refers only to the 40-sq. km (15-sq. mile) caldera at the heart of the Dyngjufjöll (a caldera is the depression caused by the collapse of the volcanic cone into the empty magma chamber). The last eruption of Askja began in October 1961 and lasted for just over three months.

A track runs from a mountain cabin on Drekagil through the lava to the edge of the huge cauldron. A further 30-minute walk along the path takes you to the **Víti** explosion crater. You can climb down the slippery slope into the crater, take a quick dip in the sulphurous, lukewarm water or swim over 'hell', the meaning of Víti. In 1875 a volcanic eruption led to the formation of a smaller crater inside the larger one, now **Öskjuvatn**, several kilometres across and the deepest lake in the country at 217 metres (715 ft).

Star Attraction
● Kverkfjöll

Below: Víti crater
Bottom: jeep in the highland snow

KVERKFJÖLL

Return about 20km (12 miles) and then cross on the F910 to the east bank of Jökulsá á Fjöllum. Soon after the bridge the route turns to the south. ★★ **Kverkfjöll** (172km/107 miles) is visible from a long way off. Reaching an altitude of 1,929m (6,328ft), this massif on the north side of Vatnajökull, situated between the two huge valley glaciers of **Dyngjujökull** in the west and **Brúarjökull** in the east, is itself split by a glacial tongue, **Kverkjökull**. Steam from hot sulphurous springs emerges from the edge of the ice or forms bizarre caves. The layout changes year by year.

To enjoy some breathtaking views over the glaciers in the south and the barren uplands in the north, it is possible, with an experienced guide, to climb over the ice into the summit region.

On the return journey to the Ring Road, you will come across another green oasis in the heart of a seemingly endless wilderness. **Hvannalindir** (200km/124 miles) was also used by Fjalla Eyvindur as a hideout.

Rejoin the Ring Road near **Mödradalur** (272km/169 miles; *see Route 4, page 57*).

Literature and Music

The poetry and prose of medieval Iceland are the country's most important contribution to European culture. The early Germanic epics such as the *Niebelungslied* have clear similarities in form, subject matter and characterisation with the Eddic poems.

The Family Sagas *(see page 13)* are magnificent stories about Iceland and Icelandic heroes from the Viking era, while the Kings' Sagas deal mainly with the background to the Norwegian rulers, but also with events in Denmark, the Faroe Islands, the Orkney Islands and the Baltic. The Icelandic sagas form the core of early medieval Nordic literature. Even during the colonial era, storytelling and the writing of prose and poetry were encouraged.

MODERN WRITERS

In the 20th century, new Icelandic writers found recognition in the English-speaking world, notably Halldór Laxness (1902–98), awarded the Nobel prize for literature in 1955. In his early years Laxness travelled widely, spending time in Germany, then in a monastery in Luxembourg, where he wrote his novel *Under the Holy Mountain* (1924), before going to Canada and the US in 1927–30. There he got involved in the Hollywood film industry and became a socialist. His writing rejuvenated Icelandic prose and he turned out a series of incomparable epic novels such as *Independent People* (1934–5), which describes the harsh conditions under which many Icelanders lived, *Under the Glacier, The Fish Can Sing* and *The Atom Station*. A book by Laxness is a good companion when visiting Iceland.

Younger writers found it hard to match up to Laxness's fame, but slowly they gained recognition and some of their works have been translated into English. These include Einar Már Guðmundsson (b. 1954; *Angels of the Universe*, 1998), Thor Vilhjálmsson (b. 1925; *Justice Undone*, 1998), winner of the Nordic Council's

Opposite: reading in a Reykjavík café
Below: Edda Manuscript
Bottom: Halldór Laxness

The Sagas in English

Many of Iceland's Sagas have been translated into English and other languages; particularly readable are Egils Saga, Laxdæla Saga and Njáls Saga, which are all published under the Penguin Classics label. The Sagas of the Icelanders, translated by Robert Kellogg were published by Viking in 2000 to commemorate 1,000 years since Leif Eriksson made his voyage to the New World. The book includes 12 Sagas, notably the Vinland Sagas. A complete translation of the Sagas in English is also published as a set – contact Mál og Menning bookshop, Suðurlandsbraut 12, 108 Reykjavík, tel: 515 2500, fax: 515 2505, e-mail: malogmenning@ edda.is; www.malogmenning.is.

Contemporary sculpture by Reykjavík's Hallgrímskirkja

prestigious literature prize, Guðbergur Bergsson (b. 1932; *The Swan*, 1998) and Einar Heimisson (b. 1966), whose novel, *Maria* (1993), now made into a film, describes the fate of Jews who emigrated to Iceland from Nazi Germany. War and its chaos also play a central role in the psychological thriller *Absolution* (1994) by Ólafur Jóhann Ólafsson (b. 1962).

The changes that occurred during the 1940s with Iceland occupied by American soldiers and subsequently forced to come out of isolation are described by Einar Kárason (b. 1955) in his brilliant trilogy *Devil's Island, The Isle of Gold* and *The Promised Land*. The books are centred on a colourful family that keeps landing on its feet. In 1992, Kárason wrote *The Wisdom of Fools*, another lively tale that follows the bizarre members of the Schrott-Fúsi family through Iceland's economic boom years. Iceland's modern poets have also been very productive and their works are published regularly.

MUSIC AND DANCE

Icelandic singers have been acclaimed in opera houses and concert halls throughout the world, but until recently little of the country's own music had reached audiences outside Iceland. Jón Leifs and Atli Heimir Sveinsson, both composers of electronic music, are well known in Europe. In the late 1970s, pop group Mezzoforte made an international breakthrough, followed 10 years later by the Sugarcubes. Their lead singer, Björk, has since become one of Iceland's most famous exports. Her albums *Debut* (1993), *Post* (1995) and *Homogenic* (1997) became world bestsellers, while *Medulla* (2004) relies mainly on voices with little instrumental accompaniment. Björk's reputation has helped move 'Ice Pop' on to the world stage, notably led by Indie band Sigur Rós.

The Icelandic Dance Company, comprising both Icelandic and foreign dancers, focuses on modern dance and has toured extensively abroad. The Icelandic Opera is a world-class professional company, featuring top performers.

The acclaimed Iceland Symphony Orchestra holds concerts during winter time only, but a vibrant music scene kicks off at the beginning of summer, both in and outside Reykjavík.

CINEMA

Icelanders are avid cinema-goers and Reykjavík has an amazing number of screens considering its small size. Most films released are from the US, though a certain number of Icelandic and European movies are also shown. There is an annual international film festival in the capital, as well as the occasional smaller festival of alternative or artistic films.

Icelandic film makers have never enjoyed worldwide box office success, but at international festivals Icelandic films regularly receive favourable reviews. The leading producer is undoubtedly Friðrik Þor Friðriksson, whose *Children of Nature* was nominated for an Oscar in 1992 as the best non-English language film of the year. With *Movie Days (1994)*, he won several awards and has enjoyed some success in Europe with *Cold Fever* (1994) and *Devil's Island* (1996) after the novel by E. Kárason. In 2000 he made a film of Einar Már Guðmundsson's *Angels of the Universe.* Shortly afterwards Baltasar Kormákur achieved justified interna-

Below: art at the Ásmundarsafn
Bottom: Listasafn Íslands

tional success with *101 Reykjavík* (2001), a zany black comedy set against the backdrop of Iceland's swinging nightlife.

OTHER ART FORMS

For centuries the written and spoken word overshadowed all other art forms. A long tradition of **handicrafts**, mainly woodcarving, is well documented in Reykjavík's National Museum. But the plastic and performing arts received little public recognition until the 20th century.

Reykjavik Art Museum

A few young **painters** and **sculptors** returned to their homeland after training at the Art Academy in Copenhagen. Jóhannes S. Kjarval (1885–1972) produced landscape paintings that attracted attention in international artistic circles. The first Icelandic sculptor of note was Einar Jónsson (1874–1954), whose home near Reykjavík's Hallgrímskirkja is now a museum. The same is true of the workshops where Ásmundur Sveinsson (1893–1982) and Sigurjón Ólafsson (1908–82) worked. The best-known contemporary painter is pop artist, Guðmundur Guðmundsson (b. 1932). Professionally he is known as Erró.

EVENTS CALENDAR

An Arts Festival is held in Reykjavík in every even-numbered year. It lasts from the end of May to the middle of June and consists mainly of plays and concerts. This biennial event is the largest, regular festival in Iceland.

In the second half of June, a jazz festival attracts an internationally acclaimed celebrity and many Icelandic musicians to Egilsstaðir (*see page 40*).

In July and August traditional riding events take place. These culminate every two years (2006, 2008, etc.) in the *Landsmót*, a sort of Olympiad for Icelandic horses.

The first weekend in August, extended by a non-working Monday, Icelanders love to get away from the towns and head for the countryside, preferably one of the few campsites in the woodland regions. If you want peace and quiet this weekend, you are most likely to find it in Reykjavík. A traditional celebration is usually held on this date in Herjólfsdalur on the island of Heimaey (*see page 50*).

Held on a Saturday in late August, the Reykjavík Cultural Night transforms the city centre into a cultural mecca, with every venue utilised. Musical events, poetry readings and street theatre are held all over the city. A fireworks display follows, and all the pubs and cafes are open late.

During the second half of September, the farmers drive the sheep and horses down from the summer pastures all together, and a colourful spectacle occurs when the stock is distributed among the various owners. To complete the celebrations, a party is held in the nearest community centre. For many rural areas, this is the most important social event of the year.

The official Christmas celebrations begin at 6pm on 24 December. Many people then head off to church before going home to a festive dinner, followed by the opening of presents and dancing around the tree. The immediate family tends to be together on Christmas Eve, while Christmas Day is typically reserved for the extended family.

On New Year's Eve there's a *brenna* – a huge bonfire lit to symbolise the burning of the old, followed later in the night by millions of króna's worth of fireworks.

Independence Day
Iceland's National Day is celebrated on 17 June, the day in 1944 when the country declared full independence from Denmark. It is also the birthday of Jón Sigurðsson, who contributed more than any other Icelander to the struggle. The greatest celebrations are in Reykjavík, with parades, street theatre and music, side shows and dancing, but throughout the country the day is a festive occasion.

Below: live jazz
Bottom: Reykjavík on New Year's Eve

FOOD AND DRINK

Icelandic specialities

Gnawing at half a singed and boiled sheep's head, known as *svið*, and taking particular pleasure over the eyes is a gastronomic experience best left to the Icelandic people. Fermented shark or *hákarl* is another local delicacy that is unlikely to whet the appetite, but for those who insist on copying the natives then it should be eaten in small bites and served with a glass of *brennivín*. Pickling in whey is an ancient form of preserving food. The result can be sampled as *blóðmör* and *lifrarpylsa*, black sausage and liver sausage made from sheep. Another example is *hrútspungur* – pickled ram's testicles compressed into a cake.

Visitors rarely encounter such unusual traditional delicacies. There are, however, plenty of Icelandic specialities that will pose no problem for the traveller keen to sample true Icelandic fare. Salted fish is prepared in such a way that hardly anyone would notice that it is not fresh. *Hangikjöt*, or hung meat, is normally smoked lamb, which can be served either as a main course or as charcuterie.

Ptarmigan, puffin and guillemot have been served on Icelandic plates for hundreds of years. *Rúgbrauð*, is a sweetish, brown to brown-black bread. Traditionally, it is prepared in a hot spring, but nowadays the dough is usually cooked by the baker in a *bain-marie*.

You will come across two types of dairy product. *Skyr* is a type of low-fat soft cheese, usually mixed with fruit or else eaten on its own or perhaps with a little milk and sugar; *súrmjólk* is the delicious thick sour milk that tastes best with brown sugar or added fruit.

In many restaurants, even outside the capital, chefs are now much more likely to experiment and prepare sophisticated food in line with current fashion. Tourists tend to prefer lamb and fish and only top quality, fresh ingredients are used. If an exotic looking deep-sea fish that you have never seen before arrives on the table, then do give it a try. When eating lamb, remember that the animal spent the summer in the uplands grazing on wild herbs, so it will not need any further seasoning.

Prices in good restaurants are consistently higher than those you are used to paying at home. A bottle of wine is likely to cost two or three times as much. Generally, fish is considerably cheaper than meat. Lunchtime meals are better value than the evening menu. Some restaurants have tourist menus or *sumarréttir* (comprising starter, main course and coffee), but it's worth asking the waiter what's on the day's menu, as it is likely to be written on a chalkboard on the wall in Icelandic.

Alcoholic Drinks

Several good varieties of schnaps, known to Icelanders as *brennivín*, are distilled in Iceland. They include the popular brand known as Black Death, which is so named because of the black label.

After the legalisation of beer in 1989, the Icelanders quickly learnt the skills of brewing. Many beers on offer are imported, but local varieties such as Egils, Viking and international brands such as Tuborg dominate the market.

The sale of alcoholic drinks, including beer stronger than 2 percent proof, is allowed only from state-run Vínbúð shops, as well as in restaurants, bars and bistro-style cafés, which must have a special licence. Opening hours were extended in 2000, with pub/club owners permitted to keep open pretty much as long as they like.

Visitors from Europe and North America will be unfamiliar with the pricing structure used in Iceland. The drinks sold in the Vínbúð shops are dear. The higher the quality, the smaller the price difference. Prices of long drinks and spirits are more in line with those of mainland Europe, while beer and wine served in restaurants are very expensive. However, most bars and restaurants have special offers on beer.

Restaurant Selection

The following are suggestions for Reykjavík and Akureyri. They are listed according to three categories: €€€ = expensive, €€ = moderate, € = inexpensive.

Reykjavík

Apótek, Austurstræti 16, tel: 575 7900. Right in the centre close to Hotel Borg, this is the place for expensive fusion cuisine. €€€

Argentína, Barónstígur 11A, tel: 551 9555. Classic steak restaurant with a cigar and cognac lounge. €€€

Café Victor, Hafnarstræti 1–3, tel: 561 9555. A lively restaurant/bar with a reasonably priced selection of dishes. Ask what's on today's menu – it will most likely be fresh fish. Situated next to the Irish pub for some lively drinking companions. €

Fjörukráin, Strandgata 55, tel: 565 1891. This restaurant is in Hafnarfjördur, south of Reykjavík. It's a taxi ride away but it's worth the effort for an unforgettable experience of a Viking-Age feast. €€€

Grænn kostur, Skólavörðustígur 8 tel: 552 2028. An inexpensive vegetarian restaurant; food is served with a hint of spice. €

Hornið, Hafnarstræti 15, tel: 551 3340. Popular pizzeria with seafood, and a cellar bar. Virtually an institution. €€

Hótel Óðinsvé, Þórsgata 1, tel: 511 6200. Run by a celebrity chef, this restaurant was recently named one of the top 100 new restaurants in the world by *Condé Nast Traveller*. The emphasis is on fish and lamb. €€€

Humarhúsið, Amtmannsstígur 1 tel: 561 3303. Romantic setting in a house that was once the home and office of the Danish king's governor. The emphasis is on lobster and fish. €€€

Jómfrúin, Lækjargata 4. tel: 551 0100. Danish restaurant that serves 120 types of open sandwiches. Best known for Saturday and Sunday brunch. €

Kaffi Reykjavík, Vesturgata 2, tel: 552 3030. Fine international cuisine, a wonderful warm atmosphere. €€

Kaffi Sólon, Bankastræti 7a, tel: 562 3232. Stylish café and bistró serving light meals and the chic set. Weekend evenings expect the beautiful crowd and great DJs. €€

Lækjarbrekka, Bankastræti 2, tel: 551 4430. In a central position, a romantic setting both inside and outside. Good value for money. €€€.

Naustið, Vesturgata 6, tel: 554 0500. Traditional fish restaurant in one of the smartest inner-city quarters. €€–€€€

Á næstu grösum, Laugavegur 20b (entrance on Suðurlandsbraut), tel: 552 8410. Small veggie and organic restaurant. €€

Þrir Frakkar, Baldursgata 14, tel: 552 3939. Neighbourhood seafood restaurant renowned for its traditional fare – and whale steaks. €€€

Tveir Fiskar, Geirsgata 9, tel: 511 3474. Fashionable restaurant noted for its fish dishes. €€€
Vegamót, Vegamótastígur 4, tel: 511 3040. International bistro serving good-quality food in a stylish environment; popular with a younger crowd. €€
Við Tjörnina, Templarasund 3, tel: 551 8666. Furnished in 1920s style, but with modern, innovative cuisine. €€€

Akureyri and Surroundings
Bautinn/La Vita é Bella, Hafnarstræti 92 (opposite Hótel KEA), tel: 462 1818. Two restaurants under one roof: La Vita é Bella is a popular Italian restaurant (€€) opening on to the fjord. Bautinn is a bistro-style restaurant with a huge choice of dishes, from salads to meat, fish and vegetarian meals. (€€)
Rósagaðurinn, Hafnarstræti 89, tel: 460 2017. Pricy resaurant in the Hótel KEA. €€€
Veitingahúsið Brekka, Brekkugötu 5, Hrísey island, tel: 466 1751 (also guesthouse). Fish restaurant on the fjord island of Hrísey. €€

Nightlife
Reykjavík has almost 100 pubs, bars and fashionable bistros. Most bars are on Laugavegur, the little side streets off Laugavegur and down the hill towards the city centre. Icelanders tend to congregate in bars around midnight and on Fridays and Saturdays clubs can stay open till the early hours of the morning.

Reykjavík's clubs
Cafe '22', Laugavegur 22, has a pub-style bar downstairs and at weekends there is dancing upstairs; popular late at night. **Café List**, Laugavegur 20, is the Spanish tapas bar in Reykjavík.

It turns wild after midnight with the art and theatre crowd. **Kaffibarinn** just up from the corner of Laugavegur 12 is a small bar popular from early evening and well into the next morning; Damon Albarn from the pop group Blur owns a stake here. Further along Bankastræti, **Prikið** finds a good balance between traditional coffeehouse and bar by day, and a busy nighttime buzz.

On the next corner down is **Kofi Tómasar frænda** (Uncle Tom's Cabin), more like Uncle Tom's basement but attracting the younger crowd who come for the beer or strong coffee. One block away at Hverfisgata 20, **Hverfisbarinn**, is one of the most popular bars in the entire city. Further down the hill, after the crossroads, you will come to **Pravda**, a busy club for those who want to be seen in the scene. Just around the corner into Austurvöllur square is **NASA**, a serious dance club and live music venue, favoured by a young, beautiful and fashionable crowd.

Across the square to the left of Hótel Borg, you'll find **Brennslan** at Pósthússtræti 9, a stylish brasserie renowned for its hundred or so different varieties of beer and a popular place for a late night tipple. Come in here and check out where the in-crowd is heading. Don't forget to pay homage to **Dubliners** just round the corner at Hafnarstræti 14, an authentic Irish pub; while **Gaukur á Stöng** at nearby Tryggvagata 22, is justifiably popular. This is the place that got the beer legislation ball rolling by serving beer cocktails. It's fun but very noisy, often with live music. While you're in this part of town, have a look, too, at **Rex**, Austurstræti 9, a trendy hangout for Reykjavík's young things, where the interior still shows remnants of the original design by Britain's Sir Terrence Coran.

ACTIVE HOLIDAYS

Riders and walkers will be in their element in Iceland, while mountain bikers can test themselves to the limit on the steep hillsides. Many glacier regions offer winter sports in the summer. Canoeing and river rafting on torrential glacial rivers are extremely popular and, thanks to the endless supply of steaming water from underground springs, Iceland is an open-air swimming pool all year.

To go **mountain biking** on Iceland's rough tracks are ideal for off-road cyclists, even though you can't cycle everywhere *(see page 112)*. Organised tours for small groups arrange for luggage to be taken ahead and the uninteresting sections are covered by bus.

Riding ranges from hour-long sessions or half-day excursions on the outskirts of Reykjavík to two-week trails through the highlands. Also on offer are upland rides, breaking in young horses in the spring, driving semi-wild horses up to the meadows at the start of summer or back down as winter approaches, etc. For further information contact **Arinbjörn Jóhannsson**, Brekkulækur Farm, 531

Hvammstangi, tel: 451 2938, fax: 451 2998, email: brekka@nett.is.

To go **walking** or **trekking**, you will need sturdy footwear, equipment that is suitable for all weathers, a high level of fitness and experience in difficult terrain. This is particularly important for the highland tours. For walking tours with Icelanders contact Ferðafélag Íslands or Útivist walking clubs *(for addresses see Cabins, page 120)*.

Winter sports are possible during the summer on several glaciers and in the Kerlingarfjöll. Winter ski areas include Bláfjöll, 20km (12 miles) southeast of Reykjavík, Hengill near the Ring Road towards Hveragerði, and Skálafell in the Esja mountains. Ísafjörður and Akureyri also have good ski areas. **Arcanum** (tel: 487 1500, www.snow.is) organises snowmobile excursions onto Mýrdalsjökull glacier.

River rafting is about gliding down fast-flowing glacial rivers in dinghies, for example on the Hvítá river below Gullfoss *(see page 37)*; day trips from Reykjavík and on rivers in the Skagafjörður hinterland *(see page 45)*. Reservations via various travel and tour companies *(see page 110)*.

White-water rafting

PRACTICAL INFORMATION

Getting There

BY AIR

Icelandair (www.icelandair.com) is the main carrier operating regular scheduled flights from Europe and North America to Iceland: (all year) London Heathrow, Glasgow, Manchester, Helsinki, Copenhagen, Oslo, Stockholm, Amsterdam, Frankfurt, Paris, San Francisco, Boston, New York, Orlando, Baltimore, Minneapolis, Madrid, Frankfurt, Barcelona, Berlin, Hamburg, Milan and Zurich.

Icelandair UK: 172 Tottenham Court Road, 3rd floor, London W1P 9LG, tel: 020 7874 1000, www.icelandair.co. uk. **US**: 5950 Symphony Woods Road, Suite 410, Columbia MD 21044, tel: 1-800-233 5500, www.icelandair.net.

The Icelandic low fares airline, **Iceland Express** (tel: 0870 240 5600 in the UK, +45 3538 3600 in Denmark, +354 550 0600 in Iceland, www.icelandexpress.com) operates from London Stansted and Copenhagen to Iceland's Keflavik airport once or twice daily depending on season (there are generally two flights a day in the summer months). You will generally find that the fares offered by Iceland Express, even in the height of summer when demand for seats is at its greatest, are consistently lower than those offered by Icelandair. Flights also from Stockholm, Gothenburg, Berlin, Frankfurt, Alicante and Friedrichshafen. British Airways (www.ba.com) operates regular flights between London Gatwick and Reykjavík. Look out also for new budget airline routes to Iceland which are likely to open up further competition between the airlines.

Iceland's international airport at Keflavík is located 50km (31 miles) from Reykjavík. A connecting bus service links the airport with the air terminal at Icelandair Hótel Loftleiðir in Reykjavík and the main long distance bus station. Onward transfer can be arranged to the major hotels.

BY BOAT

The Faroese ferry company, Smyril Line, operates a weekly service between mainland Europe and Iceland (Seyðisfjörður; www.smyril-line.fo). The ferry takes a zigzag route from Hanstholm in northern Denmark, calling in at the Faroe Islands, the Shetland Islands and Norway. Connections can be made in Lerwick, Shetland Islands, if travelling from other parts of the United Kingdom. Journey times on this route are long, however, with the voyage from London to Seyðisfjörður taking around four days.

Container ships belonging to the Icelandic shipping company, Eimskip, cover the route from Iceland to mainland Europe all year round. They carry up to 12 passengers. It is possible to send a vehicle as freight, but fly direct.

Smyril Line email: marketing@smyrilline.fo; www.smyril-line.fo. In the Faroe Islands: J. Bronsksgota 37, PO Box 370, FR-110 Tórshavn, tel: 298-345 900.

Eimskip email: info@eimskip.com; www.eimskip.com. Alternatively, contact Iceland Travel, Lágmúli 4, 108 Reykavík, tel: 585 4000; fax: 588 0202.

Getting Around

BUS, PLANE OR CAR?

Choosing which form of transport to use is no easy task, as there are many options. The choices available between Reykjavík and Akureyri, Iceland's two main towns, demonstrate the point. If you travel one way between the two towns on a scheduled bus along the Ring Road (389km/242 miles), it will cost about ISK6,600. Take the bus cross-country along the Kjölur route *(see page 92)*, then the fare will be about ISK8,000. A one-way flight at the normal tariff will probably cost less than ISK10,000; just double prices for a return ticket. Families, students and senior citizens are entitled to further reductions. A small hire car will cost anything from around ISK9,000 for a day, plus fuel. Cheaper rates for tourists apply if the car is booked for longer periods or in advance.

BY BUS

Buses run to all inhabited parts of the country. During the summer season they operate along the full length of the Ring Road every day, some sections of it several times a day. In sparsely populated regions and outside the summer season, the services are irregular. From the beginning of October until mid-May the eastern section of the Ring Road is not passable after Höfn.

A number of one-day or multi-day excursions are based around the scheduled bus services, i.e. in combination with other forms of transport (ferries, flights). If you want to rely entirely on buses, consider buying a bus pass for a full tour of the island (more expensive if including the Westfjords) or for unlimited bus travel (for one week or for four weeks) or the Highland Pass, which reduces the fares for the highland buses.

There are also many guided coach tours. Independent travellers should make further inquiries via the Icelandic Tourist Board at Laekjargata 3, Reykjavík, tel: 535 5500, www.visit iceland.com or www.icetourist.is. There are an expanding number of very good travel agencies, for example: **Destination**

Iceland, www.destination-iceland.com, or **Iceland Travel**, www.icelandtravel.is.

BY AIR

The domestic airline in Iceland is **Air Iceland**, also known in Icelandic as Flugfélag Íslands (tel: 570 3030, www.airiceland.is). Their main base is the city airport in Reykjavík, close to Hótel Loftleiðir but accessed from Þorragata off Suðurgata. Air Iceland and Landsflug (both bookable online via the former's website) operate between a dozen airports in Iceland. From Reykjavík the airline flies several times daily to Akureyri, Egilsstaðir, Höfn and Ísafjörður, while services to Bíldudalur and Gjögur in the West Fjords and to Sauðárkrókur on the north coast operate a little less frequently. From Akureyri the airlines also serves Grímsey and Þórshöfn. The Faroese airline, **Atlantic Airways** (www.atlantic.fo) flies between Reykjavík and the Faroe Islands, but it is possible to book a ticket via the Air Iceland website. Flights to Greenland are operated by Air Iceland and are also bookable online. All domestic flights, as well as those to the Faroes and Greenland, operate from Reykjavík city airport rather than Keflavík.

BY FERRY

For ferry connections *see below*. There is a connection to the Westman Islands from Þorlákshöfn (1–2 times daily; bus from/to Reykjavík). Reservations can be made at tourist information offices or via one of the many travel agencies *(see above)*.

BY CAR

Iceland's roads, once notorious for their extremely poor quality, are now mainly asphalt. Where the surface is still gravel, then drivers must, of course, take great care. Speed is the greatest risk when driving on loose surfaces. Under no circumstances should a vehicle's undercarriage clearance be restricted by overloading.

An important item for independent drivers is, of course, a good road map. The Iceland Geodetic Survey's Land-mælingar Íslands and Mál og Menning Publishers both produce maps of Iceland. These detailed maps show how the asphalting is progressing and also the ever-changing course of the highland tracks.

All the usual car hire companies have offices in Reykjavík and the surrounding area. Hertz (in co-operation with Icelandair) and Europcar have offices in other towns. Most Iceland tour operators offer car hire packages based on 100, 200 or unlimited kilometres, including fully comprehensive insurance and VAT or else fly-drive deals. Whether it is better to book in advance or when you arrive in Iceland depends, to some extent, on the current rate of exchange, but remember that during the summer not all types of vehicles are available at short notice. For travelling around the coast a normal car is perfectly adequate, but anyone contemplating a trip into the interior will need a 4-wheel-drive vehicle. (Insur-

ance companies will refuse to cover hire cars taken into the interior.)

An all-inclusive package for a smaller vehicle during the summer will cost ISK8,000–13,000 a day, a little less for an extended period; the smallest 4-wheel-drive vehicle ISK12,000–20,000 a day, again a little less for an extended hire period. One-way rentals are very expensive, unless you want an ordinary saloon car for a journey between two main towns and it is hired from one of the main companies. Many companies make a surcharge for collection/return at Keflavík airport.

Petrol is expensive in Iceland (approximately ISK130 per litre). There are plenty of places to buy fuel. Where no fuel is available for long stretches of road, roadside signs keep motorists informed. Diesel-powered vehicles are, however, heavily taxed. Tourists bringing in diesel vehicles will be charged according to weight.

TRAVELLING IN THE HIGHLANDS

The vegetation in highland areas has only two months each year to grow and so must be treated with great care. It is the duty of every traveller in Iceland to protect and to maintain the natural environment. Always stay on the beaten track. If you damage the topsoil in any way, you have created a

Cycling in the highlands

weak spot that will be exploited by the destructive power of wind erosion.

Much worse than footsteps are tyre tracks, even those left by mountain bikes. The highlands are no place for off-road enthusiasts. They should stick to the tracks – it would be hard to find tougher road conditions anywhere in Europe. Off-road driving in the true sense of the word is not permitted anywhere in Iceland. Here are a few rules to remember – most of them are just common sense.

- Leave your campsite or service area as you would expect to find it.
- Do not leave any rubbish lying around – and do not bury any either.
- Do not light a fire on vegetation.
- Do not break any stones and do not build stone figures for the fun of it.
- Do not pollute the water.
- Do not damage any plants.
- Do not disturb any animals.
- Do not alter any geological formations.
- Do not make any unnecessary noise.
- Never drive off the track.
- Always follow the signposted footpaths.

Follow the country code when hiking

- Follow the country code and the instructions of park wardens.

Fording rivers
- Check for any up-to-date information about rivers on your route.
- Never try to ford rivers in vehicles which do not have protected engines.
- If possible ford rivers in convoy, so that help is always at hand.
- Never follow vehicle tracks into a river without checking the spot first.
- Remember: fords can become dangerous at any time.
- Check the depth and current of unknown rivers before crossing.
- Wear warm, bright clothing.

To follow routes 6 and 7 *(see pages 77 and 91)* you will need a robust 4-wheel-drive vehicle with plenty of undercarriage clearance. Do not trust any notice which states that certain highland routes are passable in an ordinary saloon car. There are very few days in the year when such conditions exist and a visitor is not in any position to know for certain what lies ahead. Numerous fatal accidents occur every year as a result of visitors underestimating the road and weather conditions.

Reykjavík

The central bus stop for city buses is located on Lækjargata at the junction with Bankastræti and Hlemmur Square. One journey on an SVR bus costs 220 ISK. This has to be counted out for the driver and then thrown into a container. Long-distance buses depart from the BSÍ terminal (Vatnsmýrarvegur) on the north side of the city airport.

For a charge of between 1,200 and 2,200 ISK, the Reykjavík Tourist Card (available from tourist information offices) entitles visitors up to three days' unlimited travel on SVR buses and free admission to municipal baths and museums.

Sightseeing tours of the city and excursions into the outlying areas are provided by Reykjavík Excursions, which has an office at the BSÍ bus terminal, Vatnsmýrarvegur 10, (tel: 562 1011, www.re.is).

Akureyri
BY AIR

There are scheduled flights to Reykjavík and the island of Grímsey and to other smaller towns on Iceland's northeast coast, as well as day trips to eastern Greenland during the summer months.

BY BUS

There are buses to Reykjavík once or twice daily via the Ring Road,and in the summer also daily via the highland route; to Dalvík and Ólafsfjörður daily; to Egilsstaðir June–August, daily, mid-May–mid-October, three times a week; to Mývatn in high season once or twice daily, otherwise three times a week; to Húsavík daily, in the summer onward to Ásbyrgi (www.bsi.is).

BY BOAT

To Grímsey Island twice a week (day trip with land tour available).

Mývatn

Timetabled buses run from Reykjavík to Mývatn via Sprengisandur. Also available are excursions to the main sights around Mývatn, to Askja, Dettifoss and Jökulsárgljúfur National Park (10 hours). Ask at the tourist office or consult one of the many online travel agencies (*see page 110*).

Egilsstaðir
BY AIR

Scheduled flights to Reykjavík, Akureyri charter flights over the Eastfjords and the northern edge of Vatnajökull.

BY BUS

The Egilsstaðir–Höfn–Reykjavík bus service follows Route 5 (*see page 60*). A bus service from Egilsstaðir travels to the surrounding area, for example Hallormsstaður twice a week, Eiðar twice a week, Seyðisfjörður once or twice a day. The range of excursions for independent travellers is rather modest. However, it is possible to take combined bus/boat tours via Seyðisfjörður or Neskaupstaður to some of the more remote fjords. For up-to-date information ask at the tourist information office or where you are staying.

Höfn
BY AIR

There are scheduled services to and from Reykjavík. The airport is situated about 8km (5 miles) to the northwest of the town. Contact Flugfélag Íslands (tel: 570 3030; www.flugfelag.is) for information and reservations.

BY BUS

As well as the summer Ring Road service, buses leave daily to the main starting points for tours of Vatnajökull.

Vatnajökull

The Jöklaferðir company arranges glacier tours and excursions by snowmobile or motorised sleigh, including 1-to 2-hour trips close to the Jöklasel base on the **Skálafellsjökull**, wholeday tours and longer crossings of Vatnajökull to Kverkfjöll *(see page 97)*. For further information on any of these, and to make reservations, contact Höfn tourist information office *(see page 116)*.

Snæfellsnes
BY BUS

Buses for the Snæfellsnes peninsula leave Reykjavík every day. There are connecting excursions around Snæfellsjökull by bus or by boat around the Breiðafjörður islands.

The bus timetable in the Westfjords is restricted to only a few routes on specific days of the week. For journeys between Reykjavík and Ísafjörður, there are connections in Stykkishólmur, Látrabjarg and Hólmavík on the Strandir coast.

BSÍ Travel (www.bsi.is) arranges attractively priced package tours by scheduled bus, which include overnight accommodation, to the islands of Flatey and Látrabjarg.

BY FERRY

The *Baldur* ferry (for bookings call 438 1120, email: ferjan@aknet.is) plies the scenic route between Stykkishólmur and Brjánslækur, with a stopover on the island of Flatey 1–2 times daily; the journey time is about 3 hours. The crossing, which is part of Route 6 *(see page 77)* can be avoided, but the alternative is a 300-km (185-mile) journey along poor roads.

BY AIR

Several places along Route 6 are served by flights from Reykjavík, i.e. Flugfélag Íslands for Ísafjörður and Íslandsflug for Vesturbyggd. Flugfélag Íslands also operates a service between Ísafjörður and Akureyri. Sightseeing flights and air excursions with land tours are available to Stykkishólmur, Látrabjarg and Ísafjörður from Reykjavík.

Excursion flights to villages in the Westfjord region and to runways on the Hornstrandir peninsula from Ísafjörður are on a charter basis.

Ísafjörður

The *Fagranes* ferry (tel: 456 3155) runs throughout the year to destinations in Ísafjarðardjúp (vehicles) and during the summer to jetties on the Hornstrandir peninsula (passengers only). Motorboats are also available on a charter basis, and sometimes on a scheduled basis, to other destinations in the region. For more details, ask at Ísafjörður tourist information office *(see page 116)*.

Facts for the Visitor
VISAS

The citizens of most Western European nations, including the UK, and many other countries, such as Australia, New Zealand, Canada and the USA, need only a valid passport to enter as tourists. Details at www.iceland.is/travel-and-leisure/passportsvisas.

CUSTOMS

Clothing, equipment and vehicles for personal use may be imported free of duty. The following restrictions apply: travellers aged 20 years and over, no more than 1 litre of spirits up to 47 percent alcohol content and 1 litre of wine or 1 litre of spirits up to 21 percent alcohol content or 6 litres of imported beer.

Travellers aged 16 and over may import 200 cigarettes or 250g tobacco products, preserved food to an upper limit of 3kg per person.

Fresh food may not be imported and fuel must be stored in the vehicle's fitted tank. Fishing and riding equipment must be new or there must be documented evidence that it has been disinfected. For a small charge any equipment can be disinfected on arrival in Iceland.

TOURIST INFORMATION

In the US: 655 Third Avenue, New York, NY 10017, tel: 212 885-9700, fax: 212 885-9710, www.goiceland.org.

In the UK: there is no tourist office, but Icelandair in London *(see page 109)* and the Icelandic Embassy (www.iceland.embassyhomepage.com) provide tourist information.

In Iceland: for Reykjavík and the whole of Iceland – Aðalstræti 2, IS-01 Reykjavík, tel: 590 1550, www.visiticeland. com, www.tourist.reykjavik.is, email: info@visit reykjavik.is (June–August, daily 8.30am–7pm; September–May, Monday–Friday 9am–6pm, Saturday and Sunday 9am–2pm).

Reykjavík

There is an information desk in the new town hall, tel: 563 2005; open Monday–Friday 8.30am–6pm; mid-May–mid-September, also Sunday

Spoiled for choice in Reykjavík

noon–6pm. The following informative websites may help you plan your travels: www.discovericeland.is; www.icelandtotal.com; www.reykjavik.is; www.whatson.is; www.farm holidays.is; www.travelnet.is. Those in search of nightlife in Reykjavík should consider logging on to www.explore-reykjavik.com.

Local tourist offices

The 25-plus tourist information offices in Iceland supply information about the locality, and in some cases the whole country. They are often located in the town hall or library and many are closed during the winter. Practical information and events are shown in the free English-language leaflets *Around Iceland*, *Around Reykjavík* and *What's on in Reykjavík*, available in tourist information offices, hotels and hostels. Further details of information centres are available at www.visiticeland.com.

Akureyri: Upplysingamiðstöð, Hafnarstræti 82 (bus station), IS-600 Akureyri, tel: 462 7733; fax: 461 1817, www.eyjafjordur.is, email info@eyjafjordur.is; 1 June–31 August, Monday–Friday 8am–7pm, Saturday–Sunday 8am–5pm; winter, Monday–Friday 8am–5pm. **Arnastapi**: Snjófell, IS-355 Arnastapi, tel: 435 6783, fax: 453 6795. **Ásbyrgi**: Tjaldsvæpi Ásbyrgi campsite, tel: 465 2195. **Borgarnes**: tel: 437

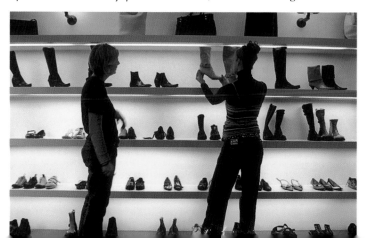

2214, fax: 437 2314, www.vesturland.is. **Djúpivogur**: Hótel Framtíð, tel: 478 8887, fax: 478 8187. **Egilsstaðir**: Kaupvangar 6, tel: 471 2320, fax: 471 1863, www.east.is; 1 June–31 August, daily 9am–6pm. **Höfn**: Travel Center, IS-780 Hornafjörður, tel: 478 1500, fax: 478 1607, www.vatnajokull.is. At the campsite. **Húsafell**: Húsafell Service Center campsite. **Hveragerði**: Breið-amörk 2, IS-810 Hveragerði, tel: 483 4601, fax: 483 4604; Monday–Friday 9am–5pm, Saturday–Sunday 10am–2pm, www.southiceland.is. **Ísafjörður**: Aðalstræti 7, IS-400 Ísafjörður, tel: 456 5121, fax: 456 5185. Monday–Friday 9am–6pm, summer also Satur-day–Sunday 10am–3pm. **Þingvellir**: Þingvellir Travel Center at the national park offices by Highway 36, tel: 482 2660, www.thingvellir.is. **Reykjahlíð**: Bjarg/Eldá Travel Services, tel: 464 4240. Tjaldsvælði Reykjahlíð camp-site, tel: 464 4103, fax: 464 4305. **Seyðisfjörður**: Ránargata 6 (by the ferry terminal), tel: 472 1551, fax: 472 1315. **Skaftafell National Park**: At the campsite, tel: 478 1627, fax: 478 1846. **Staparskáli**: Staparskáli camp-site. **Stykkishólmur**: Sæferðir, Smið-justígur 3, IS-340 Stykkishólmur, tel:

*Playing in the pool
at Laugardalur, Reykjavík*

438 1450, fax: 438 1050. The largest travel agency in the area serves both as a tourist information office and local cruise and coach operator. **Varmahlíð**: Service area (in summer only), tel: 455 6161, www.nordurland.is, email: info@ska-gafjordur.is. **Vík**: Víkurskáli service area, tel: 487 1230, fax: 487 1302.

CURRENCY AND EXCHANGE

The Icelandic unit of currency is the *króna* (plural *krónur*), sometimes abbreviated to IKr, more often now ISK. Banknotes are in denominations of 500, 1,000, 2,000 and 5,000 *krónur*, coins in 1, 5, 10, 50 and 100 *krónur*. 1 *króna* = 100 *aurar*, but the latter are usually rounded up or down and the coins are rarely used nowadays.

It is cheaper to exchange cash in Iceland than abroad. There are no cur-rency restrictions for holidaymakers and ATM cash machines are plentiful in towns. Credit cards can be used practically everywhere. Banks and larger hotels accept travellers' cheques. Credit cards are also accepted for small amounts in bars and super-markets, and even taxis. There are bureaux de change at Keflavík airport and at the ferry terminal in Seyðisfjörður. Many tourist-orientated shops accept foreign banknotes, though at poor rates of exchange.

VAT

VAT in Iceland is 24.5 percent. If you are buying high-value goods (4,000 ISK or more) in shops carrying the 'Europe Tax Free Shopping' sign, about 15 percent of the purchase price can be reclaimed. The money is returned as you leave Iceland from Keflavík airport at a branch of Landsbanki Íslands situated in the transit lounge. If you are leaving Iceland on a ferry or a cruise ship, then ask for further information from the shops participating in the scheme. Your receipt must be stamped by an Icelandic customs official. 'Europe Tax Free Shopping' has about 3,000 outlets in Europe, from which the rebate can be collected.

PUBLIC HOLIDAYS

New Year's Day, Maundy Thursday, Good Friday, Easter Sunday, Easter Monday, first day of summer on the third or fourth Thursday in April, Labour Day (1 May), Ascension Day, Whit Sunday, Whit Monday, Icelandic National Holiday (17 June), Shop and Office Workers' Holiday on the first Monday in August, Christmas Eve from noon, Christmas Day and Boxing Day, New Year's Eve from noon.

TELEPHONE AND FAX

When making calls within Iceland, simply dial the seven-figure number. There are no area codes. When calling Iceland from Europe, prefix your number with 00 + 354. When dialling home from Iceland, start with 00, dial the country code (e.g. UK = 44, US and Canada = 1), then the area code without the 0, followed by your number. International calls can be made from all telephones. Phone cards are available from post offices.

GSM mobile phones can be used as long as you have had the international roaming bar lifted. Reception is possible in all but the most remote areas of the country.

POSTAL SERVICES

Most towns have a post office and telephone booths *(Póstur og Sími)*, open Monday–Friday 8.30am–4.30pm. The rate for letters and postcards to Europe is 60 ISK.

TIPPING

It is usual to offer a small gratuity to the drivers and guides responsible for sightseeing tours.

TIME

GMT applies throughout Iceland all year round.

ELECTRICITY

The voltage in Iceland is 220V. Continental-style sockets and plugs are used, so adapters are needed for UK and US plugs, and transformers for US 110V appliances.

OPENING TIMES

Shop opening times are largely unrestricted. Most open Monday–Friday 9am–6pm, Saturday 10am–4pm. Kiosks at petrol stations in rural areas sell a wide range of goods and stay open late. Banks open Monday–Friday 9.15am–4pm. There are extended opening times at Keflavík airport and the tourist information office in Reykjavík (Aðalstræti 2).

SOUVENIRS

Classic souvenirs from Iceland are wool and woollen products in traditional or modern designs, made from the soft and water-resistant wool of the Icelandic sheep. The best place to buy such items is one of the shops belonging to the rural women's co-operative. Craft shops often sell innovative jewellery, glass and ceramic pieces.

Clothing and Equipment

Wind- and rainproof jackets and trousers are essential. Take at least one pair of shoes or walking boots that cover the ankles. Rubber sandals or an old pair of trainers and a telescopic walking pole are helpful when crossing rivers. If you intend to camp, take the best-quality sleeping bag, tent and insulated ground mat you can get.

Traffic Regulations

Icelandic traffic regulations are basically the same as the rest of Europe. Signs are few and far between but, where they do exist, they must always be heeded, particularly the one marked *Blindhæðir*, which warns of blind spots on narrow roads. The maximum speed in towns is 50km/h (30mph), outside built-up areas on gravel roads 80km/h (50mph), 90km/h (55mph) on asphalt roads. Seat belts must be worn front and back and headlights switched on at all times. Drink-driving laws are strictly enforced. The blood alcohol limit is 0.05 percent. When animals and cars meet, the vehicle driver is liable to compensation claims by the owner of the animal.

Photography

Films for cameras and video equipment are widely available, but expensive. Some museums forbid photography. It is illegal to photograph protected birds in their nest.

Medical

Medical provision in Iceland is very good. All larger towns have hospitals or health centres. Look in the inside cover of the telephone directory under *Læknavakt* (emergency doctor) and *Sjúkrahús* (hospital).

Health and Insurance

Visitors to Iceland should take out medical insurance that will meet the full extent of any claim. Travellers from EU countries can present the European Health Insurance Card (details at www.ehic.org.uk), which entitles them to the benefits of the Icelandic health service at the same rates as Icelanders. However, this usually involves a hefty private contribution, e.g. for dental treatment and medication. Tap water is safe to drink.

If you are bringing your car to Iceland, you must insure against salvage and transport costs. Even write-offs have to be exported or incur heavy import duties.

Emergency Numbers

Emergency *(Neyðarsími)*: tel: 112. Other numbers on the inside cover of the telephone directory: Fire *(Slökkvistöð)*; Police *(Lögregla)*; Ambulance *(Sjúkrabíll)*; Emergency doctor *(Læknavakt)*; Hospital *(Sjúkrahús)*.

Lost and Found

Ask at the nearest police station

Visitors with Disabilities

In remote areas accommodation and facilities adapted for people with disabilities are not generally available.

For information on planning a trip contact the Association of the Disabled in the Capital Area, **Sjálfsbjörg**. Hátún 10, 105 Reykjavík, tel: 530 6700, fax: 530 6701, www.obi.is. **Ferðafélagar hf, Reynigrund** 65, IS-200 Kópavogur, tel: 564 4091, fax: 564 4092, runs tours for disabled groups.

Diplomatic representation

United Kingdom: Laufásvegur 31, tel: 550 5100, www.britishembassy.is.
US: Laufásvegur 21, tel: 562 9100, www.usa.is.
Canada: Túngata 14, tel: 533 5550, fax: 533 5551.

ACCOMMODATION

Iceland has more than 100 hotels and guesthouses, ranging from simple country hotels and boarding schools converted into hostels to luxury accommodation with all mod cons. In addition, there are over 100 farmhouses, 26 youth hostels, 34 mountain cabins belonging to both hiking clubs, countless sleeping bag cabins for backpackers and more than 120 campsites. Some hotels and guesthouses have cheap dormitories with either made-up beds or mattresses for sleeping bags.

Accommodation vouchers are not always better value than cash. As it is not possible to make advance reservations with vouchers, they are not a lot of use if at the end of a long day's hiking, the hotel for which the voucher is valid has no beds. Unused vouchers are normally only reimbursed at 80 percent.

Hotels are priced as follows: €€€ expensive; €€ moderate; € basic.

HOTEL CHAINS

Fosshótels, Skipholt 50c, IS-105 Reykjavík, tel: 562 4000, fax: 562 4001, www.fosshotel.is. Good tourist hotels of varying standards – 12 in total though a few are only open in summer. **€–€€€**

Icelandair Hotels, c/o Hotel Loftleiðir, IS-101 Reykjavík, tel: 444 4000, www.icehotel.is. Eight comfortable hotels open year-round. **€€–€€€**

Edda Hotels, tel: 444 4000, www.hoteledda.is. A chain of nice hotels around the country. Some are open year-round, others open summer only. A few are operated in boarding schools that are on vacation. **€–€€**

Kea Hotels, Hafnarstræti 87–9, 600 Akureyri, tel: 460 2000, fax: 460 2060, www.keahotels.is. A chain of five reasonable and comfortable hotels across Iceland, open all year round. **€**

GUESTHOUSES

These offer an inexpensive alternative to hotels, mainly in the towns (usually €). Generally only breakfast is available, though it is not always included in the room rate.

FARMHOUSES

Farmhouses provide bed and breakfast and other meals on request. Farm guesthouses are listed in the Icelandic

Gardening on Austurvöller, Reykjavík

Farm Holidays booklet, available through tourist offices and tour operators, which also handle bookings, or direct from **Icelandic Farm Holidays**, Síðumúli 13, 108 Reykjavík, tel: 570 2700, fax: 570 2799, www.farmholidays.is.

YOUTH HOSTELS

Youth hostels accept all guests with no age limit. Among the 26 hostels (most open only in summer) are farmhouses, clubhouses and schools, all with cooking facilities. Many offer double rooms, but combined accommodation for men and women is the rule rather than the exception. The atmosphere is relaxed. An overnight stay costs from 1,700 ISK per night for Youth Hostel Association members. Bed-linen, available for hire, or a sleeping bag are required. Information from Bandalag Íslenskra Farfugla, Sundlaugarvegur 34, IS-105 Reykjavík, tel: 553 8110, fax: 588 9201, www.hostel.is.

CABINS

Free sleeping-bag cabins (for backpackers) are as varied as youth hostels; not all have cooking facilities. Non-members of the two organisa-

Statues outside Perlan, Reykjavík

tions listed below may use **hiking club cabins** in the interior. These mattress camps cost £10–£15 ($18–30) a night. It is best to bring your own food and a stove.

In summer, booking and pre-payment are essential, through the club offices: **Ferðafélag Íslands** (Touring Club of Iceland), Mörkinni 6, 108 Reykjavík, tel: 568 2533, fax: 568 2535, www.fi.is; **Útivist**, Laugavegur 178, 105 Reykjavík, tel: 562 1000, fax: 562 1001, www.utivist.is. Orange emergency cabins are privately owned and not for tourists' use.

CAMPSITES

Campsites can be found in almost every district, in all national parks and near popular sightseeing areas. Camping is permitted only within fenced-off or attended spaces, subject to the landowner's agreement. Camping is often free at the most basic of sites; otherwise, expect to pay around £10 (€18) per person per night. A list of campsites is available from the Icelandic Tourist Board *(see page 115)*.

Hotel Selection

The following are suggestions for the main destinations in this guide. They are listed according to three categories:

€€€ = expensive, €€ = moderate, €= inexpensive.

Reykjavík

Grand Hótel Reykjavík, Sigtún 38, tel: 514 8000, fax: 514 8030, email info@grand.is. Comfortable hotel with spacious rooms and excellent service. Located close to the Laugardalur swimming pool. **€€€**

Guesthouse Baldursbrá, Laufásvegur 41, tel: 552 6646, fax: 562 6647. One of the best guesthouses in the city. Friendly service and a hot tub in the back yard. **€€**

Hótel Borg, Pósthússtræti 11, IS-101 Reykjavík, tel: 551 1440, fax: 551 1420; www.keahotels.is. The city's first hotel, right in the old town centre. Beautifully renovated in Art Deco style. **€€€**

Hótel Klöpp, Klapparstræti 26, Reykjavík, tel: 511 6060, 511 6070, www.centerhotels.is. This is a pleasant new hotel conveniently set in the town centre. The nearby Hótel Skjaldbreið (Laugavegur 16) is run by the same company. **€€€**

Radisson SAS Saga, Hagatorg, tel: 525 9900, fax: 525 9909, www.hotel saga.is. A top-class hotel not far from the city centre and next door to the University Theatre. One of the best restaurants in the country on the top floor. **€€€**

Icelandair Hótel Loftleiðir, v/ Hlíðarfót, tel: 444 4500, fax: 444 4501; www.icehotel.is. A 220-room hotel near city airport; business/conference facilities. **€€–€€€**

Guesthouse Adam, Skólavörðustígur 42, tel:896 0242, email: adam@ adam.is. Good location close to the Hallgrimskirkja; open all year. Breakfast is not included. **€€**

Ísafold, Bárugata 11, tel: 561 2294. Centrally located and convenient. It has comfortable, individually decorated rooms. **€€**

Reykjavík Youth Hostel, Sundlaugavegur 34, IS-105 Reykjavík, tel: 553 8110, fax: 588 9201, www.hostel.is. Well-run hostel with good facilities. Often noisy in the morning as guests leave early. Good position near swimming pool, but 30 minutes' walk from the centre. **€**

Room With a View Apartments, Laugarvegar 18, tel: 552 7262, www. roomwithaview.is. Penthouse apartments on the main street in the centre of Reykjavík. Great view over the city; some apartments have access to a jacuzzi on the balcony. Can accommodate 1–7 persons.

Salvation Army Guesthouse, Kirkjustræti 2, tel: 561 3203, fax: 561 3315, www.guesthouse.is. This is the most inexpensive guesthouse in Reykjavík. Basic, but neat and clean, with cooking facilities. Located right in the town centre. **€€**

Akureyri

Hótel KEA, Hafnarstræti 83–85, tel: 460 2000, fax: 460 2060, www.hotelkea.is. Undoubtedly the best hotel in Akureyri in terms of service and location though the rooms are somewhat dull. A very reliable hotel in the centre of town. **€€€**

Hótel Norðurland, Geislagata 7, tel: 462 2600, fax: 462 7962, www.hotelkea.is. Comfortable, but rather ordinary hotel near the town hall square. **€€€**

Hótel Harpa, Hafnarstræti 83–85, tel: 460 2000, fax: 460 2060, email: harpa@keahotels.is. Sharing the same facilities as the Kea but cheaper and a little less luxurious. **€€**

Hótel Edda, Eyarlandsvegur 28, tel: 461 1434, fax: 461 3033. Older summer hotel near the pool. **€–€€**

v/Þórunnarstræti campsite, tel: 444 4900. Centrally located near the swimming pool. Lively, sometimes rather loud.

Arnastapi
Guesthouse Snjófell, IS-355 Arnastapi, tel: 435 6783, fax: 453 6795, www.snjofell.is. Accommodation (with space for sleeping bags), restaurant, tourist information and excursions. **€**

Ásbyrgi
Tjaldsvæfi Ásbyrgi, IS-641 Húsavík, tel: 465 2195. The National Park runs two campsites here. The one at the entrance is very well equipped, the other rather basic. **€**

Borgarnes
Hótel Borgarnes, Egilsgata 14-16, IS-310 Borgarnes, tel: 437 1119, fax: 437 1443. Pleasant, upmarket hotel with good restaurant. **€€**
Hyrnan campsite near the petrol station on the edge of town. Brúartorg, IS-310 Borgarnes, tel: 430 5550, fax: 430 5551. Modern service area, with wide range of 24-hour facilities including cafeteria. **€**

Breiðavík
Breiðavík, Látrabjarg, IS-451 Patreksfjörður, tel: 456 1575, fax: 456 1189. Basic summer accommodation in an old boarding school; small cafeteria. **€**

Breiðdalsvík
Hótel Bláfell, IS-760 Sólvöllur 14, tel: 475 6770, fax: 475 6668. Rooms are of varying standard; space for sleeping bags. The restaurant has received international awards. **€€**
Berunes Youth Hostel, Berunes 1, 765 Djúpivogur, tel: 478 8988, fax: 478 8902, email: berunes@simnet.is. Pleasant hostel in an old farmhouse. **€**

Djúpivogur
Hótel Framtið, Vogarland 4, IS-765 Djúpivogur, tel: 478 8887, fax: 478 8187. Friendly hotel in an old Danish trading centre; space for sleeping bags; fish restaurant. **€€**

Egilsstaðir and environs
Hótel Hérað (Icelandair Hótel), tel: 471 1500, fax: 471 1501, www.icehotels.is. Modern (1998), upmarket hotel open all year. **€€€**
Edda Hótel, tel: 471 2775, fax: 471 2776. The house next door offers basic rooms during the summer months. **€–€€**
Campsite, tel: 471 2320. Noisy campsite near the shopping centre and service area. Waste-disposal facilities.
Gistiheimilið Eiðum, IS-705 Eiðar, tel/fax: 470 0750. Basic summer hostel in Eiðar's primary school 12km (7 miles) north of Egilsstaðir, with the choice of double or family rooms. **€**
Hótel Edda Eiðar, tel: 444 4870, fax: 444 4871. Boarding school summer hotel; indoor pool and restaurant. **€**
Hússtjórnarskólinn, IS-707 Hallormsstaður, tel: 471 1763. Summer hotel, basic rooms in old college. **€**
Fosshótel Hallormstaður, tel: 471 1705, fax: 562 4001. Summer hotel in woodland setting near the Lögurinn lake. **€–€€**
Atlavík campsite, Hallormstaður. Idyllic lakeside spot in the woods.
Skipalækur (west of the Largarfljót bridge), tel: 471 1324, fax: 471 2413. Tourist-style farm accommodation with 80 beds in various buildings and cabins; horses for hire, and snow scooters in winter. Fishing permits for sale. **€**
Farfuglaheimilið Húsey, Tunguhreppur, IS-701 Egilsstaðir, tel: 471 3010, fax: 471 3009. Nearest shops in Egilsstaðir. **€**

Flatey
Veitingastofan Vogur, tel: 438 1413. This is basic summer accommodation with space for sleeping bags and a cafeteria. **€**

Goðafoss

Gistihúsið Fosshóll, v/Goðafoss, IS-645 Fosshóll, tel: 464 3108, fax: 464 3318. Farmhouse accommodation close to the Goðafoss. Made-up beds, hostel with space for sleeping bags, well-equipped campsite and all-day cafeteria. **€**. Locally-run co-operative sells handicrafts.

Grindavík

Northern Light Inn, tel: 426 8650, fax: 426 8651, www.nli.is. The only hotel close to the Blue Lagoon. Transfers can be arranged to and from Keflavík airport. **€€**

Hellissandur

Hótel Edda, tel: 444 4940, email: hellisandur@hoteledda.is. This modern hotel parallel to the main road offers the best accommodation in town. Open from mid-May to September. **€€**

Höfn

Stafafell í Lón, IS-781 Höfn, tel: 478 1717, fax: 478 1785. Farmstead with youth hostel, farmhouse accommodation, space for sleeping bags and campsite. Jeep tours to the hiking areas in the hinterland. **€–€€**

Icelandic horses

Hótel Höfn, tel: 478 1240, fax: 478 1996, www.hotelhofn.is. Central hotel equipped with all modern conveniences. **€€€**

Ásgarður, tel: 487 8367, fax: 487 8387, www.geysir.com/asgard. New resort with camping and cottages. **€€**

Hótel Edda Nesjaskóli, tel: 444 4000. Typical summer hotel with space for sleeping bags, about 7km (4 miles) outside the town near the airport; coaches and scheduled buses from and to the west stop here. Open mid-June to mid-August only. **€–€€**

Gistiheimilið Hvammur, Ránarslóð, tel: 478 1503, fax: 478 1591. This is an eight-room pension close to the harbour. **€**

Well-equipped campsite on the outskirts of town by the Travel Centre. Tel: 478 1000, fax: 478 1901.

Húsafell

Húsafell Service Center, tel: 435 1550, fax: 435 1551. Well-equipped campsite and basic hostel (**€**) adjacent to a geothermally heated swimming pool.

Húsavík

Fosshótel Húsavík, Ketilsbraut 22, IS-640 Húsavík, tel: 464 1220, fax: 464 2161. Modern and functional accommodation and facilities. **€€€**

Árból, Ásgarðsvegur 2, tel: 464 2220, fax: 464 1463. Pleasant bed and breakfast, close to the town centre. **€**

Hverageröi
Hótel Ork, Breitumörk 1c, IS-810 Hveragerdi, tel: 483 4700, fax: 483 4755. Luxury hotel on the outskirts of the town. Excellent restaurant and thermal baths. **€€€**

Hveravellir
Ferðafélag mountain cabins by Hvítárvatn and in Hveravellir. Also campsites.

Hvolsvöllur
Hótel Hvolsvöllur, Hlíðarvegur 7, IS-860 Hvolsvöllur, tel: 487 8050, fax: 487 8058. Convenient hotel with restaurant, open all year round. Close to the Saga Centre. **€–€€**

Ísafjörður
Hótel Ísafjörður, Silfurtorg 2, tel: 456 4111, fax: 456 4767, email: info@hotelisafjordur.is, www. hotelisafjordur.is. Central, modern hotel with good restaurant. **€€€**
Framhaldsskólinn campsite, tel: 456 4485. Space for sleeping bags in an edge-of-town boarding school. **€–€€**

Stylish bar in Reykjavík

Kirkjubæjarklaustur
Hótel Kirkjubæjarklaustur (Icelandair Hótel), Klausturvegur 6, tel: 487 4900, fax: 487 4614. Summer hotel with space for sleeping bags **€–€€**; plus more comfortable hotel wing, open all year; pool and restaurant. **€€€**

Laugarvatn
Hótel Edda Íkí Laugarvatn, tel: 444 4820, fax: 444 4821. The more comfortable of the two Edda hotels in the town; restaurant. **€€**

Lýsuhóll
Lýsuhóll farmhouse, Staðarsveit, IS-355 Ólafsvík, tel: 435 6716, fax: 435 6816. Space for sleeping bags; whirlpool with spring water available for guests. **€**

Mývatn
Hótel Reynihlíð, 660 Reykjahlíð, tel: 464 4170, fax: 464 4371. Lake Mývatn's top hotel; popular restaurant, which can get busy with coach tours. **€€€**
Hótel Reykjahlíð, tel: 464 4142, fax: 464 4336, email: reykjahlid@ islandia.is, www.reykjahlid.is. Fully renovated hotel, with nine comfortable rooms; restaurant. Magnificent lakeside position. **€€**

Guesthouse Stöng, tel: 464 4252, fax: 464 4352. A farmhouse about 10km (7 miles) from the southwestern tip of the lake. Space for 50 guests, meals available. **€**

Skútustaðaskóli, tel: 464 4279. Basic summer accommodation in a school; lots of space for sleeping bags. **€**

Bjarg/Eldá Travel Services, tel: 464 4240. Private bed and breakfast (**€**) and popular campsite by the lake. Open 15 May–30 September. Used by many independent travellers, Eldá organises round trips and sells tickets for tourist amenities provided by other companies.

Tjaldsvæði Reykjahlíð, tel: 464 4103, fax: 464 4305. Well-equipped campsite, popular with groups. Space for sleeping bags in huts. Open 1 June–10 September.

Nýidalur

Ferðafélag mountain cabins by the main route and by Laugarfell (with hot pool) by the F752, 30km/19 miles to the northwest towards Varmahlip.

Ólafsvík

Hótel Ólafsvík, Ólafsbraut 20, IS-355 Ólafsvík, tel: 436 1650, fax: 463 1651, email: hotelo@simnet.is. A 14-room guesthouse with restaurant on main street; can arrange glacier tours. **€**

Þingvellir

Hótel Valhöll, tel: 486 1777, fax: 486 1778, www.hotelvalholl.is. Traditional hotel below Almannagjá rift by lakeside. Summer only. Good restaurant serving fresh trout. **€€–€€€**

There are several campsites in the National Park.

Reykholt

Hótel Reykholt, IS-320 Reykholt, tel: 435 1260, fax: 562 4001. Summer hotel in a modern boarding school. **€**

Reykir

Sæberg, Reykir, IS-500 Brú, tel: 451 0015, fax: 451 0034. Friendly and inexpensive hostel. **€**

Reykjadalur

Narfastaðir, tel: 464 3300, fax: 464 3319. Farmhouse accommodation with over 50 beds. **€–€€**

Fosshótel Laugar, tel: 464 6300, fax: 562 4001. Summer hotel in a boarding school featuring thermal baths and restaurant. **€**

Reykjanes

Ferðaþjónustan Reykjanes, IS-401 Ísafjörður, tel: 456 4844, fax: 456 4845. Spacious complex with rooms, space for sleeping bags and camping area; many activities. **€**

Hótel Djúpavík, 522 Árneshreppur, tel: 451 4037. Basic hotel in an old hostel for workers at the fish factory. **€**

Staðarskáli

Staðarskáli, IS-500 Staðarhreppur, tel: 451 1150, fax: 451 1107. Away from service area. Some basic rooms, plus pleasant country-style restaurant. **€–€€**

Sauðárkrókur

Fosshótel Áning, v/Sæmundarhlíp, 550 Sauðárkrókur, tel: 453 6717, fax: 453 6087. Modern, well-equipped summer hotel with excellent restaurant. **€€**

Selfoss

Hótel Selfoss, Eyrarvegur 2, IS-800 Selfoss, tel: 482 2500, fax: 482 2524. Modern business hotel in town centre; restaurant. **€€€**. About 100 metres away, the more basic **Hótel Þóristún,** is under the same management. **€€**

Hótel Geysir, IS-801 Selfoss, tel: 486 8915, fax: 486 8715. Hotel with space for sleeping bags. **€**

Seyðisfjörður

Hótel Snæfell, Austurvegur 3, tel: 472 1460, fax: 472 1570. Timber house in town centre. Friendly ambience. Only 9 rooms. Restaurant (**€€€**) serves good fish. **€–€€**

Farfuglaheimilið Hafaldan, Ránargata 9, tel: 472 1410, fax: 472 1610. Rather primitive hostel with dormitory accommodation. **€**

Skaftafell National Park

Hótel Skaftafell, Freysnes, IS-785 Fagurhólsmyri, tel: 478 1945, fax: 478 1846. Functional but pleasant hotel with space for sleeping bags in an annexe. Just under 4km (2½ miles) east of the National Park; facilities include restaurant. **€€**

Hof í Öræfum, IS-755 Fagurhólsmýri, tel: 478 1669, fax: 478 1638. Farmhouse located 20km (12 miles) from Skaftafell National Park. There is also sleeping-bag accommodation. **€–€€**

Well-equipped campsite near service centre. Tel: 478 1627.

Skógar

Hótel Edda Skógar, tel: 487 4900, fax: 487 4614. Old school building between the museum and waterfall. **€**

Taking a break in Lækjartorg

Stykkishólmur

Fosshótel Stykkishólmur, Borgarbraut 12, 340 Stykkishólmur, tel: 430 2100, fax: 430 2101. Sombre appearance compensated for by a great view; restaurant. **€€€**

Hótel Eyjaferðir, Aðalgata 8, tel: 438 1450, fax: 438 1050. Central position. Make reservations via Eyjaferðir travel agency. **€€**

Varmaland

Varmaland Guesthouse, tel: 435 1303, fax: 435 1307. Hostel-style accommodation in a location near the Ring Road. **€**

Varmahlíð

Hótel Varmahlíð, IS-560 Varmahlíð, tel: 453 8170, fax: 453 8870. Small hotel with restaurant, open all year round. **€€**

Vík í Mýrdal

Hótel Vík, Klettsvegur, tel: 487 1480, fax: 487 1302. New hotel near service area. **€€**. Large campsite opposite Víkurskáli service area, tel: 487 1345, or make reservations through tourist information office.

Guesthouse Norður-Vík, Mýrdal, 870 Vík, tel: 487 1106; fax: 487 1303. This is a basic hostel located just outside Vík. **€**

INDEX

Accommodation ..119
Aldeyjarfoss 94
Álftafjörður 64
Akureyri 47–50
Almannagjá gorge ..38
Almannaskarð pass 64
Arnarfjörður 87
Arnastapi 80
art 102
Ásbyrgi gorge 56
Askja caldera.........97
Austurhorn 64
Berserkjahraun 83
Berufjörður 62
Bláa Loníð.............25
Bogarvirki fortress 45
Borgarnes 77
Breiðafjörður.........84
Breiðárlón glacial
 lake 67
Breiðavík.............86
Breiðdalsvík 62
Búðir 79
Cape Bjargtangar...86
cinema 101
climate 11
Dalatangi 61
Dettifoss 54
Dimmuborgir.........52
Djúpavík 90
Djúpivogur 62
Drangey island 46
Drekagil gorge....96–7
Dritvík 80
Dynjandi waterfall..87
Dyrhólaey 71
Economy 14–15
Egilsstaðir 58
Eiríksjökull 44
Eldborg volcano ...78
Fagurhólsmýri 67
festivals 102–3
Fjarðará canyon69–70
Flatey island 84
flora and fauna 11–12
Geography 9–10
geology 8–9
Glaumbær
 Folk Museum 45
Goðafoss 50, 94
Grábrók crater 44
Grenjaðarstaður Folk
 Museum 54

Grímsey island 50
Grímsstaðir 54
Grjótagjá caves 53
Gullfoss 37, 92
Hafnarfjörður 32
Hallormsstaður 58
Hamarsfjörður ...63–4
Hamarsrétt............45
Heimaey island ..74–5
Hekla volcano 35
Hellisgerði lava park
 32
Hellissandur 81
Hellnar.................80
Hengifoss 59
Herðubreið volcano
 95–6
Hindisvík seal bay ..45
history 18–19
Hjálparfoss 36
Hjörleifshöfði 71
Hnjótur folk museum
 85
Höfði woodlands ...52
Höfn 64
Hofsós 46
Hólar 46
Hólmavík 90
Hóp tidal lake 45
Hrafnseyri vicarage 88
Hraunfossar 43
Húsafell 43
Húsavík 54–5
Hvalfjörður 42
Hvannadalsshnúkur 67
Hveragerði............34
Hverarönd geothermal
 field 54
Hverfell 53
Hveravellir 93
Hvítárvatn glacial
 lake 93
Hvítserkur 45
Hvolsvöllur 73
Ingólfsshöfði island 67
Ísafjörður..............88
Jökulsárgljúfur
 National Park 56
Jökulsárlón lake......66
Jökulsá á Brú river 57
Katla volcano 70
Kerið crater 34
Kirkjubæjarklaustur 69

Kirkjufell 82
Kjölur plateau 92
Krafla 54
Kverkfjöll massif...97
Lake Mývatn 51
Laki crater 69
Landmannalaugar ..73
Langjökull 43, 93
language 14
Látrabjarg cliffs.....86
Laufás local history
 museum.............50
Laugavatn 37
literature 99–100
Litlanesfoss 59
Lögurinn 58
Lómagnúpur 68–9
Lóndrangar 80
Lúdent 53
Lundey island 56
Maritime Museum 89
Mjóifjörður 61
Möðrudalur 57, 97
Morsárjökull 68
Mount Helgafell ...83
music 100–1
Mýrdalssandur.......71
Námaskarð 54
nightlife 107
Núpsstadur farm ...69
Nýja-Eldhraun
 lava field 69
Olafsvík 82
Öxarfjörður inlet ...56
Papey island 63
people 10, 12–13
politics 17–18
Prestagil ravine 61
Pýrill mountain 42
Restaurants 106
Reykholt 42–3
Reykir 44
Reykjafjörður 87
Reykjahlíð 53
Reykjanes peninsula 89
Reykjavík 22–3
Sagas 17
Sænautasel farmhouse
 57
Sauðárkrókur.........46
Selfoss 57, 73
Seljahjallagil gorge 53
Seljalandsfoss 72

Seljavellir 72
Seyðisfjörður.........59
Sigulfjörður...........46
Skaftafell
 National Park 46
Skálafellsjökull 45
Skálholt 64
Skeiðarársandur.....47
Skógafoss 49
Skriðuklaustur 40
Skrúður bird rock ..43
Skútustaðagígar
 pseudo-crater 36
Snæfell 41
Snæfellsjökull
 volcano 78
Snæfellsnes peninsula
 78
Sólheimajökull 71
Sprengisandur 93–4
Staðarskáli 44
Steingrímsfjarðarheiði
 plateau..............90
Stöðvarfjörður 62
Stóragjá caves 53
Stóri-Geysir...........37
Strandir coast.........90
Strokkur geyser 37
Suðurnes (Reykjanes)
 33
Stykkishólmur 83–4
Súgandisey island ..84
Svartifoss 67
Tourist information
 115
Varmahlíð 45
Varmaland.............44
Vatnajökull 59–60, 66
Vattarnes lighthouse 62
Viðimyri church 45
Vigur island 89
Vík í Mýrdal 71
Víti crater 97
Westman Islands 74–5
whale-watching 54, 82
Þingeyri 87
Þingvallavatn.........38
Þingvellir 38
Þjóðveldisbærinn
 Viking house 36
Þjórsárdalur 35
Þórisvatn 38
Þórsmörk Valley ...72

Register with
Hotelclub.com/insight-guides
and get **£10** OFF
your next hotel booking!

Great hotels, great rates, 365 days a year

At HotelClub.com we reward our members with discounts and free stays in
their favourite hotels. As a Member, every booking made by you through
HotelClub.com/insight-guides will earn you **Member Dollars**.
When you register, we will credit your account with
£10 FREE Member Dollars, courtesy of *Insight Guides* and *HotelClub.com*

With great savings of up to 60% on over 30,000 hotels across 120 countries,
over 5 million members already use **Member Dollars** to pay for all or part
of their hotel bookings.